Merry Christmas 2001

The Rules of the Game

TO

Chad and Mandi

They know why.

Contents

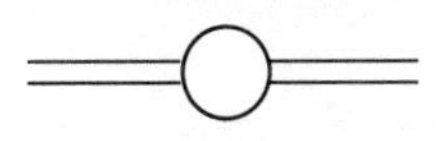

INTRODUCTION

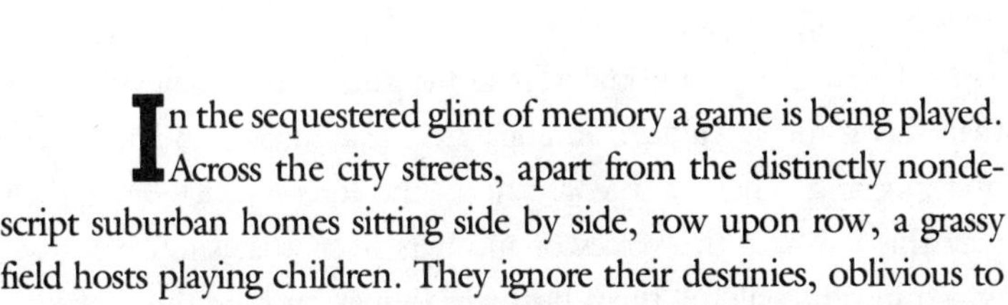

In the sequestered glint of memory a game is being played. Across the city streets, apart from the distinctly nondescript suburban homes sitting side by side, row upon row, a grassy field hosts playing children. They ignore their destinies, oblivious to events that await them, darkly, brightly. There are no boundaries to the field until it stops abruptly at streets on two sides, a graveled alley to the rear. A brick church, austere and unadorned, guards the left-field line.

The children have shed coats and sweatshirts and created a crude base path. Home plate is a red jacket, bright and alluring. First and third, in clearly unequal distances from home, are blue and black pullovers, having seen their better day. Black third base, closer to home than to first, has been placed in its location by a young boy who, surveying the distances, realizes that an accurate placement would put the sweatshirt squarely in a mud hole created by last night's rain. Hoping later to reach that pinnacle, the boy has chosen safe sliding over the exactitude of geometry.

Second base, nearest the alley, is still unsettled. It is being placed by committee who, first arguing over distance and then location, finally compromise and drop the green sweatshirt in a spot that creates, from above, a diamond cut by an amateur.

Teams begin to divide, not unlike an amoeba splitting in two. Two boys, probably the oldest, split off in separate directions and choose, one by one. Slowly a milling mass becomes two smaller masses, clutching after gloves and balls and bats, taunting and bantering at each other, planning their heroic deeds in their heads—for in their heads all is success.

No one argues over home team as the game begins. They all know that this game is endless, innings are meaningless, and the score unimportant. Their only constraints—the forces which limit their play this day—are the voices of mothers from that suburban row, which in time will call them home to dinner, picking them off one by one until, their ranks depleted, the game fades quietly away into the dusk of evening.

None will remember the score—or more likely, everyone will remember it differently, each player's young memory sharp with his own hit, pitch, or catch. Eventually the memories dull and fade into some other activity, some other time, only to be renewed when someone shouts again, "Let's play ball!"

Like these children, my memories of baseball began on the grassy churchyards and were eventually promoted to the regulation infields, with genuine backstops, of Nebraska. It is now a distant recollection, etched long ago on a glass which has been clouded by other, more significant experiences. I struggle to remember my teammates, my coaches, the positions I played, the nature of the game as I played it.

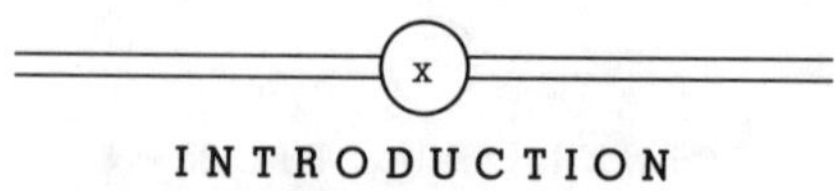

In recent years my own experiences were renewed by new and fresh experiences of my own children, who now place the bases under the cottonwoods and pick the teams, and who now dream the dreams.

And through that renewal comes an awakening of lost feelings. First in the gut, then the chest, then slowly and imperceptibly in the mind, until the embellished memories of my own days in the sunlit infields have become inexplicably and wondrously intertwined with those of my offspring. Memories lead to reflection, reflection to knowledge, knowledge to understanding. The game, still innocent yet for us, has at the same time for me become a simile, a metaphor, a proverb, a psalm. Which leads me to where I am today.

In years past I played on the field, like my son and daughter, carelessly naive about what it meant. In months past I coached their teams, still learning the lessons taught by the game.

Now, I can only dream of the grassy fields, the smooth white skin of a new ball, the smell of an old glove too worn out to keep but too much like an old friend to throw away. I am ages away from the two-out doubles that rally the team from behind, the gut-wrenching heroics of a tired but determined boy throwing his heart out, the pickoff play conceived in the devious eyes of the catcher and cunningly executed on the unsuspecting base runner. I am far away from all that.

My story is a long one, with chapters unfinished and mysteries still to be explored. It rises up at me like a blizzard, unexpectedly furious, and slaps at my psyche like icy winds and sleet and snow. Since this book is about baseball, not me, it is enough to say that in January 1993 I was a lawyer, a county attorney, a Nebraska state senator, a Little League coach, a husband and father. By October of that year I was where I am now—in prison—serving time, years of time, for theft, and my status as all but a father, which I guess you can only lose voluntarily, is over.

The story of my fall is for another place, another time. But the consequences of my fall, the tumultuous reversal of the values that I had instilled in my children, turned upside down by my actions, are not delayed and therefore the story of that reversal cannot be postponed.

Children are dramatically more honest than adults. My own son and daughter, with their hurting eyes and quavering voices, have asked me how this happened. In doing so, they have opened up a chasm of bigger questions. Standing next to it, and looking across to them, it seems impossible to ford, too wide to bridge, too deep to explore. So I look for a pathway between my misdeed, my broken values, and their need to understand.

The pathway is the place where I came as a child and return as an adult, the place where they followed as children and where they will return as adults—the place where I hope to find mutual understanding. A place born of mighty dreams grounded in dirt and elevated by the sweet smell of freshly cut grass. A place that cared for me in years past when my own life felt out of balance and confused. The place: Little League.

So, as I did when I was a child and as I did again as a father with my own children, I return to the fields and playgrounds of Nebraska, in hope of finding not victory or glory, nor hits and homers, but simply the childlike honesty that is the essence of baseball. I search to find that essence of the game we played long ago, the game I lost, and the game I seek again to play today. That endless game we play until darkness calls us and we drift slowly off, one by one, to our homes.

1

ROUGHED UP IN THE FIRST

You must try to generate happiness within yourself. If you aren't happy in one place, chances are you won't be happy in any place.

Ernie Banks

I'd seen enough. I moved from the hard white seat in the dugout to the short, railroad tie wall between home and third and back to the dugout again. The scorebook showed a base on balls to the sixth man in the lineup, walking in a run. Now the pitcher was behind the number-seven man, a weak-hitting left fielder whose halfhearted swing at the first pitch, a low, outside ball, had brought his near-apoplectic coach out of the third-base box, vehemently giving the take sign again and again. The next three pitches were balls, thrown hard but with no real idea of where they were going, like the wild swings of a tired and stunned boxer fighting his way out of a corner. The count was 3 and 1.

J. C. was our most reliable pitcher. He was big for his age, thirteen, and his tall, rangy body made him look much older. He had the exterior toughness that comes naturally to some boys who grow up alone, either absent a parent or with parents too preoccupied with their own lives to devote the time necessary to make a difference in his. His attitude on the mound was surly and angry, and he threw the ball hard, like he hated it in his hand. When J. C.'s turn to pitch came, catchers, usually anxious to be the center of the action, acquired abnormal desires to play other positions for which they were ill suited. It hurt to catch J. C.'s fastball.

A fastball was all he had. No change-up, no curve, no slider. Just pure, raw speed. He could throw hard and throw well, and once in a groove, you could count on two hands the number of pitches he'd throw in an inning. Batters feared him, and an occasional errant throw, over a head, at the belt, down in the dirt, was enough to convince most who faced him that self-defense, not contact, was the ultimate victory.

But not today. Today was different. It might have started in the warm-ups when he threw a ball too hard while shagging flies in the outfield. It might have started even earlier, as he drank an ice-cold Coke and inhaled two red dogs with cheese and onions before the opening pitch. Or it might have started earlier than that, early in the morning or late last night, when some hidden event occurring far from the field triggered an emotion in his psyche that stayed with him, acting unconsciously to throw off his rhythm. It mattered little where or when—it was clear that it had happened. And there was nothing that could be done except watch and hope, suffering along with J. C. the public embarrassment he faced in his lackluster performance.

He'd walked the first batter on six pitches, all hard fastballs, placed injudiciously in six different places. I was not so sure the batter had even seen them, but the umpire had. The second batter, a wisp of a boy with a uniform that fit like it was his older brother's, had watched that display, and when his turn at bat came, he looked over to his coach for a reprieve. The coach clapped his hands, encouraging action, and started through a series of signs so intricate the boy grew wide-eyed watching.

Did I see him cross himself? the batter wondered. *That sign I understand.* He stepped into the batter's box, gingerly positioning himself as far away from the plate as the chalk line allowed.

"C'mon, J. C., rock 'n fire, buddy!" I yelled.

The catcher, my son, put one solitary finger down between his shin guards. Fastball.

J. C. uneasily adjusted his hat, pulling it down over his forehead to shade his eyes from the afternoon sun now high above the grandstand directly behind home plate. His windup was mechanical, unnatural, and he stiffly pushed off his left leg, whipping his right arm and releasing the ball toward home. It sailed errantly inside, and before the batter could escape, it struck him in the small of his back, now turned and exposed to the hard white weapon.

"Take your base," the umpire offered first as a condolence.

The boy, stunned and hurt, stumbled down to first as his coach jogged over to talk.

"You okay, son?" asked the coach, calling time. He rubbed the spot on the boy's back, which was just beginning to get red. Tomorrow, the boy would proudly lift up his shirt and show his friends the roundish black-and-blue memory, laughing and bragging, "Naw, it never even hurt a bit." Today, however, it clearly did.

Wiping a tear from his eye, he said simply, "Yeah."

I'm not sure that hitting that boy didn't hurt J. C. just as much. He'd been there before, and he remembered how it hurt. He took something off the next two pitches. Once the batter realized what was happening, he sent the third pitch hard into left field, moving the base runners over and filling the bags.

A Little League coach is given few true opportunities to impact a game with his coaching, his knowledge of the game, and his ability to move his team. It is on tension-filled occasions such as these, a game hanging in the balance, when a coach usually saunters out to the troubled and desperate pitcher to offer the words of experienced wisdom that will undo the damage evident at all corners. I divulge this conversation against my better judgment.

"J. C., how's your arm?"

"It's fine."

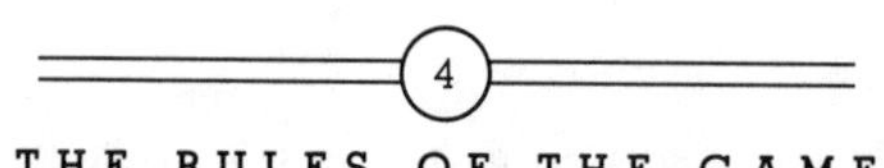

"Can you throw a strike?"

"Yup."

"Well, now's a good time."

"Okay."

As you can tell, the words, like pearls, fell from my tongue.

J. C., obviously inspired, responded by walking the next three batters on twelve pitches. Two of the boys appeared not to breathe during their at bats. One looked like he had his eyes closed. The umpire, awake, saw it all. I watched J. C. struggle, pitch after pitch. His teammates' confidence buoyed mine, though my face, grimacing after the third run had walked in, betrayed my concern.

One more batter, I said to myself.

The count quickly ran to 3 and 1, familiar territory, and I called time. Behind the plate the umpire raised his arm; play stopped and the infield relaxed into an uncomfortable anticipation. Again I went to the mound.

"J. C., you look tired."

Beneath the bill of his cap, sweat beaded off his brow and rolled into his eyes, which were moist.

"M'arm's sore." That was a sign to me that did not register.

"This is the number-seven man. Just throw strikes and get us out of here."

"Okay." J. C. put the ball back into his glove and turned back to the rubber and dug at it with his cleats as I turned away.

It was simple. Just throw strikes.

The next pitch, thrown at about half-speed, was watched by the batter into the catcher's well-worn glove, his pud.

"Strike!"

"Nice pitch, J. C.! C'mon, J. C., one more! He's a looker, J. C.!" The infield, moments ago lethargic and despairing, had come alive.

J. C. cloned another pitch at the batter. Backed into a 3–2 corner, the batter swung, shocking his coach who had given him the take sign. Now, I don't particularly like take signs for Little Leaguers. You can't learn to hit watching pitches, especially on 3–2 counts. Only this time, as the bat made solid contact and shot the ball off into right center, I sort of wished the boy would have caught the sign. The ball evaded the center fielder with a skip and a bounce and rolled unaccosted to the fence. Triple. We were down 6–0. I'd seen enough.

Having to pull your ace pitcher in the first inning is like putting an unwanted baby up for adoption. At the time, it looks like the best thing to do, but you hope that you won't decide later that you wish you had kept him. For today, J. C. was done. With a pat on the rear, I sent him to third base, making the change. Hey, the kid can still hit.

After the game, in which we staged a valiant but short-lived comeback and lost 7–5, the team met under the light pole near left field. It was tradition to do that, win or lose. We talked about the spirited comeback, sparked by a single hit by the lead-off man and a triple by J. C., and about how we stayed in it with good defense. But the hole we had dug early was too much to overcome. J. C. winced at that and hung his head.

"We play again Tuesday. Just be ready to play at the start next time, boys. Every game starts with the first pitch," I counseled.

"J. C.?" I stopped talking and looked at him.

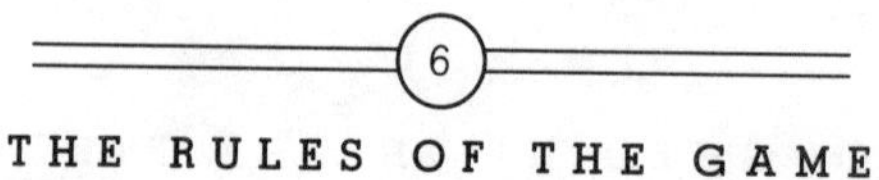

He looked up, eyes glistening under his hat.

"You're pitchin'."

Somewhere, at this moment, across the Nebraska plains in a backyard, a young child and a parent begin to play catch. The child holds the too-big glove on his hand, outstretched, while the parent tosses the soft safety ball underhand toward the glove. Missed. Again, underhand to the glove, hitting the webbing and out onto the soft green grass. This time, the ball sails straight up and the parent retrieves it. Methodically, this parental attempt at the small success of the first catch can go on for hours, days, weeks. Sooner or later the ball softly thrown lands in the glove and the too-small free hand clamps down over it, trapping forever in leather and love the sweet, satisfying moment of a child's first catch.

This is work, often tedious and unrewarding. Most parenting is. Yet it is every bit as necessary as the difficult work done by a builder when he digs deep into the ground to lay a foundation. Once completed, the foundation is never seen again. It is buried under sand and dirt, covered with layer after layer of heavy block, designed to support the whole base. It will only be noticed again if it's defective.

As we look for answers, for solutions to the mysteries of raising children, we need to recognize the familiar as a way to build a foundation that will support our children throughout the epic shifts they will inevitably face in their lives. With baseball, the simple, purely American game of baseball, parents are afforded an opportunity to play with their children and, at the same time, teach them the rudimentary and the subtly discovered lessons of life.

Watch even the youngest child after being given a ball for the first time. A bond forms as soon as the young hand can begin to grasp the ball. While the first throw may be awkward, the basic motion is there. Even a child who cannot yet walk to retrieve the ball wants first to throw it. Someone need only be on the other end to catch it.

Nothing about baseball is easy. Neither is raising children. The beauty of baseball is that in learning the game and teaching it to our children, we begin to realize how complex the lessons and how intricate your involvement in the teaching must become to be successful. Baseball is a hard game to play, a harder game to truly understand. In the difficulty lies the achievement. If, as a teacher and a player, we can master the rules and techniques of baseball, the nuances and ingenuity of hitting, pitching, and fielding, there is little else we cannot do.

Baseball, however, is not like piano. It can't be learned alone; it is designed to be interactive. You can throw a ball up in the air to learn to catch a pop fly, but it is not the same as jumping at the crack of a bat and settling under the ball in an open field. You can go to a batting cage and take a hundred cuts, but until you've looked in the eyes of the opposition on the mound and convinced yourself of his humanity, you'll never hit the ball with confidence. Baseball, like life, is best if experienced with others: fathers and sons, mothers and daughters—any combination will do. Parent and child is my personal favorite.

I began coaching Little League in order to spend more time with my children. In our little community, during the summer months, we eat, sleep, and live baseball. Games for both boys and girls occur five nights a week, and tournaments of some sort are held nearly every weekend. Endless hours are spent practicing fielding and hitting, preparing for the games, taking care of the field and concession stand, coaching, and attending the games. To say that summer baseball consumes our little town of Homer like a patch of blue in a Nebraska sky would not be an exaggeration.

After the games, parents and children hash and rehash each game, inning by inning, on the ride home over country roads, dust kicking up behind the truck in the warm, moist summer air.

And during that drive home, with the windows down and the radio silent, your son's or daughter's sweaty, dirt-stained face shining in the dim amber glow of the dashboard, you begin to realize that your reflection in the mirror isn't the one that matters. Slowly, imperceptibly, like the corn growing and maturing in the fields you pass, you begin to understand that most of your life is not your own. Other people and events intercede in it, usurping its self-importance, bringing a fear that the time has already passed for you to make a difference.

All of which brings me back to the game and the first inning. My love of baseball, especially Little League baseball, stems partly from my belief that the game, when properly taught and understood, becomes under analysis more than a game. The game becomes an analogy—or rather a hundred analogies inside another analogy. Little League is much more than a simple game played by young children. The essence of Little League, stripped away from the hard-core competitiveness of overwrought parents and coaches, is simply that all of life's lessons (or at least those that merit learning) can be taught and learned within the confines of a ball diamond in a small-town ballpark on a sunny summer afternoon.

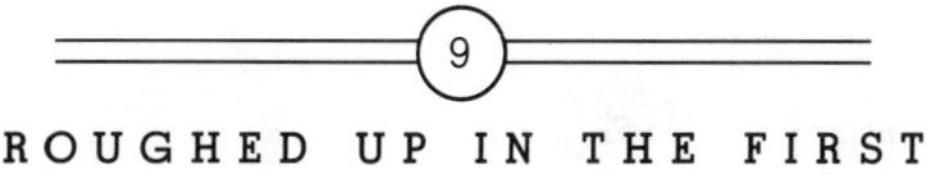

J. C., our pitcher, was what we would call "roughed up in the first inning." Discouraged, out of pitches, beaten almost before he started, he could not finish the game he had started so full of promise.

It is not uncommon for kids to get roughed up in the early innings—in the game and elsewhere. Intentional and unintentional wrongs, neglect and avoidance, presence and absence, all of these play a role in the development of our children. In their early innings, the early years, teaching and learning and nurturing are as essential to the development of proper emotions in a child as water, fertilizer, and sunshine are to the normal growth of a stalk of corn. Absent elements stunt growth, cut short promise.

Baseball reeks with clichés. We are bombarded by them during every interview at every post-free-agency signing of a million-dollar-contract prima donna mired in a .230 hitting slump. I avoid them as best I can, but since they are part and parcel of baseball, to some extent they are unavoidable.

It is not a cliché, however, to say that a father or mother, preferably both, who care for and nurture their children, is vital to the healthy, emotional development of the psyches of those children. A child without that will develop some shortage, which will either remain short or be overcompensated for in another, unbalanced way. The obligation of a parent does not stop at procreation but starts there, and it continues and intensifies as the needs of the child increase.

Yet despite our best intentions, there is on occasion little we can do to prevent our children from getting kicked about emotionally at some point early in their lives. It's unavoidable and to some extent not entirely undesirable if handled with care, like a short-hop grounder to second. The ball, hit hard in the dust, doesn't always roll true and easy into the fielder's glove, often unexpectedly taking a wild carom into the unprotected chest of that unprotected child. When that happens it hurts, and there is not much you can do but put your arm around that child's shoulder and say how proud you are that he kept the ball in front of him. It won't end the pain, but kids are tough and resilient about that kind of thing, and if given a reasonable explanation of why it hurts, and why it's okay to hurt once in a while, they will understand enough to ease the pain, at least until the bruise appears.

Little League in the last few years has taught me some valuable lessons, which I, by coaching and playing baseball with my son and daughter and the sons and daughters of others, have begun to understand and appreciate differently. It is essential for me to explore this though, because I do not yet comprehend what I believe I know. I am convinced that a good deal more than fielding and hitting and throwing, winning and losing, failure and success can be learned on the grassy diamonds of America, where young children in their innocence pick teams, lay out the boundaries of the game, and play effortlessly until time and darkness call them away.

Oh. You ask how J. C. did when he pitched again Tuesday?

He did fine.

2

THE BALLPARKS

God makes a home for the lonely;
He leads out the prisoners into prosperity,
Only the rebellious dwell in a parched land.
Psalm 68:6

A ballpark at night is more like a church than a church. . . . An empty ballpark at night must be like the inside of a pyramid.

W. P. Kinsella, *Shoeless Joe*

Across America, in the big cities and their outlying neighborhoods, in villages and country towns, there exists in each a common feature tucked away in a small corner field or prominently displayed as the crown jewel of public pride. The ballpark.

Ancients, practicing phrenology on a community, could discern the character of its people by touching, feeling, and observing the geographic bumps, humps, and swells of its public places of recreation. It is no exaggeration to say that a community is either dead or dying if it has not provided for its children public space to play baseball.

In my own community of Homer, where I once lived, the baseball field, once active as a hotbed of the amateur art of town-team baseball, then suddenly dormant, has seen a recent revival. Locals, seeking the return of a ballfield they remembered as children, have begun to toil again at the task of returning the park to its former honored status.

Set eastward, with a backdrop of tree-covered shale bluffs jutting upward, the park is a natural amphitheater for the exploits of youth. The backstop bluffs drop into a flat, rocky surface, which serves as a foundation for the semicircular grandstand. Wooden benches bolted to concrete steps seat more people. The grandstand is crudely covered by a wooden, green asphalt-shingled half roof, a friend against the summer suns and the unpredictable thunderstorms that roll over the bluffs and onto the field. To each side of the grandstand a gentle hill rolls lazily down to the flat, brown field which stretches out down first and third, safe, like a pudgy mama's arms.

The field was once a county fairground where stables and outbuildings stood and where 4-H'ers showed cows and horses and rabbits to the delight of their parents. Each August the fairground offered summer respite from day-to-day drudgery with contests and prize livestock and cotton candy. Now the stark and flat field moves out to an undefined line where infield ends and outfield begins, marked by encroaching not-grass in a wildly undulating arc behind the dirt.

The outfield grass, in need of a mowing, sweeps under a chain-link fence and into another park. The field is not level; a six-foot outfielder looks five-five at the deepest part of center field. On the lines, atop the fence, orange posts mark the outer limits, sentries to the foul ball.

Years ago, the high school shop class made signs that were fastened to strategic placements in the outfield—left center: "275"; dead center: "325"; and right field: "225." A good left-field pull hitter can nearly reach the roof of the Methodist church beyond the right field, and despite the legends passed around between cups of joe at the local cafe, no one ever has.

The field is like the thousands of other fields that dot the American landscape. And like a snowflake or a fingerprint, it is unique, with its own indelible and remarkable image. This field, so similar, yet so individual, plays tricks on all who venture to master the game and learn its secrets.

It was hot, oppressively hot, as the boys took to the field, languid and sticky. The afternoon sun hung high overhead, like a heat lamp over an incubator, and reflected its rays off the hard brown surface into the players' young faces.

The first baseman, a hefty boy who had shaved his head at the start of the season and kept it smooth with his dad's razor, drew his hand over the glistening stubble then replaced his hat. He carried a ball in his glove as he approached first, stepped on the bag, then turned and threw the ball along the ground to his infield teammates for warm-ups.

The pitcher, lithe and wiry, massaged the mound with his cleats, then set up to play catch with his catcher. They tossed the ball, oblivious to everyone else, in mock formality.

In the outfield, a new ball was thrown high into the air from right to center to left, then back again.

Three separate and distinct choruses on the field, each with its own cadence, practiced basic technique in an easy, relaxed manner, yet on the edge of uneasiness, knowing that soon practice would end.

The warm-up balls were tossed toward the bench where a boy wearing a poorly fitting hat gathered them up, putting one in his glove and the others in a ball pile near the end of the bench. A dim hum of chatter began as the catcher, stifling in sweaty armaments, announced, "Coming down!" The catcher caught the last warm-up pitch and threw it to second, one-hopping it into the second baseman's glove who put the imaginary tag on the base runner and started the ritual toss around the horn.

Home-field advantage on our small-town field carried little meaning, except that most of the town kids could walk to the ballpark. The field offered that advantage but took away some others because of its prior life as a fairground. The field was more like an archaeological dig than a ballpark. Throughout the game one player after another would stoop over to pick up a rock, a pebble, a nail, or a nut and toss it off the playing surface. This had been going on for years, and still, with each new drag of the infield, more rocks were exposed and disposed of. Infielders, alert to the dangers of a small pebble or rock in the path of an oncoming grounder, carefully manicured the field before them.

The grounders to second and short, having the farthest distance to travel and thus more opportunity to be waylaid off course, were the most difficult to handle. Usually we assigned two seasoned players, the surest hands, to these positions, and today was no different. Travis took short. Ryan took second.

Travis, light and quick and athletic, could move with unusual deftness for a boy of fourteen. He was speedy and reliable; his throws to second and first were generally on target, even if a bit tentative. Ryan, smallish and fragile-looking, had an inner toughness that belied his exterior. He was the kind of boy you wanted playing second base. Both boys appeared ready in warm-ups to handle the hits that might come their way, but neither could anticipate the mystery or, on this day, the mastery the field would have over their apparent readiness.

One of the axioms of baseball is its consistent inconsistency. On the Little League fields, untouched by the modern science of manufactured turf, every hit is different, every roll unique. Practice can teach experienced positioning and technique but only raw reaction can regularly turn that into success. Each ballplayer must react in a split second to a multitude of variables to complete a play. That ability to react through experience—an ability that cannot be taught—must be learned in order to smoothly field and cleanly play the shots hit throughout the game. This day, under the swelter of the sun, the lessons would come the hard way.

The visitors, a Little League team from a nearby town, wore green and gray uniforms that bore the various names of sponsors on their backs: feedlots, auction barns, local banks, and insurance agents. This team came from cattle country, but their town business owners were smart enough to know where their bread was buttered. Smartly attired, the team nonetheless looked overmatched. They had had but one base runner, on a walk. But, hoping to incite a rally, he had started late from first to steal second and had been promptly picked off by a nice throw from my son, Chad, who was catching behind the plate. Any parent wells up with pride at the good play of her or his child. I am no different. A knowing glance and a clenched fist pumped at him after the play assured him of that.

Trouble didn't start until the fourth inning when we held a comfortable 4–0 lead. All appeared in hand; hitting, pitching, and fielding had all been steady. Suddenly, without explanation or reason, things went from great to god-awful.

Their first batter in the fourth, who struck out swinging in the first, appeared to pose little danger. He swung at the first pitch, a low fastball, and topped it past the pitcher toward Travis, who reacted to the crack of the bat by crouching and waiting. The ball, slowed by field friction, took a hop off some unseen artifact, glanced off Travis's shoulder, and fell harmlessly to his right, the damage done. Single.

The next batter, swinging late at each pitch, nevertheless connected weakly on a grounder tailor-made for a 4-6-3 double play. Just as the ball skidded into Ryan's glove, dutifully placed flat on the ground, it took a hop, defying any known law of physics, or at least any law Ryan knew, hitting the heel of his glove and jumping between his legs onto the outfield fringe. Single.

This comedy was not funny to the players who were being taken by this turn of events where they wished not to go. As I watched those field events unfold, the best I could advise was "Get in front of it, Travis," as if the ball hitting his shoulder was some indication he was not, and "Watch the bad hop, Ryan," as if my telling him publicly to do exactly what he had tried to do would somehow make it easier. I knew that at that moment if good advice was like manna from heaven, our forty-year walk in the wilderness was going to leave some very hungry refugees. Mercifully though, both boys nodded at my sage advice, and I was spared from knowing what they really thought of my comments.

The game grew even more aberrational after that. A high fly ball, easily catchable in short center field, was lost in the sun, and it dropped aimlessly in front of the bewildered, blinded boy. A wild pitch scooted past Chad, careened wildly off a railroad tie wall behind the plate, and before it could be retrieved, the base runner had advanced two bases. A short pop fly was lifted to right field, and as the right fielder settled under it, the ball hit a light pole along the line and was ruled out of play. A shot, pulled hard down the third-base line, was nearly smothered by the edgy third baseman before it hit the bag, shot skyward into left field, and died in the tall grass. The left fielder finally realized what had happened and found it and relayed it back into action.

When the boys finally got the inning's third out, they came back into the dugout, unbelieving, shell-shocked like a cadre of wounded doughboys.

"Man, I shoulda had that ball at third. I can't believe it hit the bag!"

"You shoulda played over."

"What, and stand on the bag? It won't hit the bag again like that in a hundred years."

"Did you see it stop?"

"I can't believe I didn't make that catch in the outfield! I just lost it in the stinkin' sun."

"Want to use my glasses? They just flip down."

"I had that foul before it hit the post. That was a sure out."

"Hey, get your pitches up a little. If it hits the backstop again, who knows where it will go!"

And so, on it went. Just the natural banter of young boys trying to fathom the unfathomable, trying to make sense of the nonsensical reality of one inning in one game. What they did not understand was that placement, precision, and practice would have been of little help to them. None of those can darken the sun, move a light pole, or remove the rough edges of a field on which they play the game. You play the game where you play the game, accepting the uneven ground, tall grass, the misplaced pole, the short fence, all of those as they are. You accept that which you cannot change and adapt as best you can to the confined boundaries of the field of play.

Some people are drawn to nature's creative monuments—the deep canyons, the rock formations, the soaring mountains, the variant rivers and streams. Others prefer man's own creations—the skyscrapers, the suspended bridges, the architectural wonders that cover the landscape. When I travel, I am invariably drawn to the combined natural and human-made creations, part grass and earth, part wood and steel, designed and constructed by the hosts of volunteers who tirelessly toil in constructing Little League parks.

It is easy to tell a park cared for and constructed with funds raised by candy sales and Friday-night fish frys and pancake breakfasts from one constructed with federal grant funds. One park is begotten in true need and constructed by loving volunteers on harried weekends; another is designed in sterile offices and subbed out to specialists. One park exists—the other breathes. One sits in perfect mathematical congruity, a multiplex, diamonds back to back, arranged in a gaudy setting, like the ring of a cheap thrill. The other, arranged with first one diamond—the crown jewel—then another as kid demand and time and pancake proceeds permit. They are arranged with care and originality like a well-lived-in family room.

Many towns boast with justifiable pride about their field. I have seen many and loved a few, but one field near my home in Nebraska stands out as special. Up in the northeast corner, where the gentle hills begin to roll into the bluffs and then into the bottomland of the Missouri River, sits the town of Wakefield.

In the Midwest, towns proclaim special distinctions for themselves and exhibit public pride in some special feature, some attraction: "Kolache Capital of Nebraska." "Sausage Capital of the West." "Home of Buffalo Bill." "Biggest Little Town in Three Counties." The proclamations are endless and colorful.

Wakefield has taken on the ostentatious title of self-proclaimed "Baseball Capital of Nebraska." On the outskirts, south of town, where the two-lane highway has run past a new housing development, the main business district, the grain elevators, well drillers, and gas stations, the sign sits big as life. It shows an overly large map of Nebraska with a big baseball in the northeast corner. Someone has attached a small sign below the billboard announcing the week in October to honor the pumpkin, but that event is a weak sister to the ringing proclamation: "Wakefield—Baseball Capital of Nebraska." They wouldn't say it if it weren't true.

Each summer after the local crops are laid by and the first cutting of alfalfa is safely put up, Wakefield suspends its other normal activities for two weeks and organizes a tournament for the young boys and girls of the area. They begin playing on three separate fields early on a Saturday afternoon. Teams from all over the area bring their boys and girls to play, and during those two weeks baseball reigns over crops, weather, and farm markets. The tournament is organized by volunteers, run by volunteers, played on fields built and maintained by volunteers, and their love for the game and the kids that play it is evident and bountiful.

Each team and each player is announced over loudspeakers before every game at each field. For some kids this is the first time they have heard their names called that loudly without having them followed by parental discipline. Each player, before each game, recites the baseball pledge, an oath to themselves and the fans, as a reminder of the spirit in which they participate in the game.

> I promise that I will:
> Keep the rules.
> Keep faith with my teammates.
> Keep my temper.

Keep myself fit.
Keep a stout heart in defeat.
Keep my pride under in victory.
Keep a sound soul, a clean mind, and a healthy body.

Good plays are rewarded with intelligent applause from knowledgeable fans and fun commentary from announcers. Players' names are announced again at each bat, and occasionally a parent or coach or kid will politely correct the announcer's pronunciation, who then good-naturedly corrects himself amidst the laughter.

"Batting now, number fifteen, playing shortstop, Jim Krauss!"

"Krau-see! Krau-see!"

"Excuse me, Jim Krau-see!"

Excellent offensive and defensive plays are rewarded by a gift certificate redeemable for a soda at the local shop downtown. The kids often wonder what they did that was so outstanding to deserve the award, but they never turn down the soda.

Each field is uniquely designed for each age group. The youngest play on a shortened version with a nearly reachable fence. The middle group on a slightly larger field. And the oldest on the large diamond, with a grass infield, warm-up alleys, discrete protective fencing, full night lights, a real wooden outfield fence, and an irrigated and manicured turf.

And something else. Something almost forgotten by the modern ballfield designers. Dugouts. Honest-to-big-league, three-concrete-step, full-block-back, wooden-roofed, wooden-floored, bench-worn-smooth, ground-level dugouts. If you can't spit sunflower seeds in a place like that between plays and action and baseball lies, you can't spit them anywhere.

It is incredible to watch a boy transformed as he steps onto that field like a warrior into an arena. Young, unsure of himself. Then suddenly wise, confident, and cocky on it. For a moment, before all that can go wrong in a game and destroy the aura of invincibility and damage the ego, each boy believes he can do it all. He becomes a ballplayer, an exceptional playmaker, unmarred by the outside, in a world unto himself. All is within his easy grasp. Once past the metal gates of the field through which only players and coaches are admitted, a player leaves behind his brother or sister, his parents, unfinished business, unmade beds, unmowed lawns. All that matters in this realm into which he and his teammates step, bonded together, baseball blood brothers, is the game.

Teams I have coached have won and lost on that field—lopsided victories that were never in doubt and heartbreaking losses that stung like sweat in your eye. But I do not recall one boy ever sorry he played the game on that field.

I can't say the bad hops are less regular or the sun somehow not as blinding. Even the dugouts, while much beloved, create a new and unexpected obstacle to catching a foul ball. The distance from home to first is the same as elsewhere. The batter's box there looks like the batter's box anywhere else. Yet this field is somehow different, more forgiving than others.

Perhaps it is because this field carries with it the heart of a town that cares deeply for its kids. More than anything, the people who built and care for this field want a place where kids can play and learn the game they love. In their toiling they create an atmosphere.

The field on which the game is played is important, but a field without a town's love is a close relative to a bare acre of land—productive, possibly, but ultimately as forgettable as yesterday's forecast.

Kids will play the game anywhere you allow them. From town to town, field to field, they will field the balls, catch the flies, and swing at pitches about the same no matter where the field lies. They'll take the good hops with the bad, complain about the uneven mound or crooked foul lines, but nonetheless they'll play, resigned to that over which they have no control.

And while every field is the same, every field is different. We can't eliminate the uneven play nor should we seek to. Uneven play teaches character, and the game's bad bounces create in each participant a respect for the nature of the unexpected. So we should seek a field on which our children can learn the game and take its bounces. It doesn't need to be perfect. All we need is a diamond that is tended to by adults who seek to make a place to learn and play the game of baseball, adults who put themselves equally into the task of raising their children—adults like those in the town that declares itself with the justifiable pride of a loving parent, "Baseball Capital of Nebraska."

3

JASON GETS A HIT

Ted Williams is the man who always said that hitting a baseball was the toughest thing in sports. And I'm a disciple who says that hitting a baseball when you're coming off the bench, bottom of the ninth, against somebody throwing heat or split-fingered magic, is the toughest part of the toughest thing. But it's still better than lifting things.

Jay Johnstone, *Temporary Insanity*

Satisfaction is the grave of progress.

Anonymous

It was a late Tuesday afternoon. We were scheduled to play another small-town team, this time from Emerson. When Nebraskans say small town, they mean it. Homer residents number under six hundred, Emerson slightly over eight hundred.

As we prepared to bat in the late innings against the team from Emerson, the world again compressed so that all that mattered, the only destiny that drew near, was confined to the field where once again two sets of young boys played baseball.

An intense rivalry between these towns and these teams was born of parents who had played each other on these fields. The rivalry always burned hot when these teams from these towns were cast against each other on a field of contest. Despite that rivalry, these boys thought it was just another game. As they grew older, their parents and fans would explain all the past contests, and they too would learn the rivalry. They too would discover their own flame. Now, this was just another game with just another team.

The game as it started was presumed innocent. Early in the first inning, Homer had started a rally. With no outs, Travis had walked, stolen second, then advanced to third on an infield hit legged out by Eric. Long and lanky, Eric more loped than ran, and he covered ground in a surprisingly generous gait. Once at first, with Travis still at third, Eric promptly stole second without a throw from the catcher, since he knew a throw to second, possibly successful, would surely allow the runner at third to advance and score.

With third and second full and first open, their pitcher, a small left-hander with a deceptive delivery, walked Drew on six pitches. Our cleanup batter, J. C., was up, with Chad, just as proficient, to follow.

The pitcher, whose brother was a star in high school and was watching from the stands, threw a slow, lazy curve, and J. C., anxious, swung so hard it nearly screwed him into the ground.

"C'mon, J. C., be patient," I yelled. "Wait on it."

The base runners sneaked small leads, unused to the pickoff move possessed by the wily hooker. The second pitch looked low but was called a strike. J. C. stepped out of the box. His eyes met mine, looking for an answer.

"That's two on you. Nothin' close now. Little contact stroke now, little single."

He nodded once, acknowledging my encouragement, spit, put his right foot into the box, and dug in for the pitch. Another curve. J. C., wiser, waited and then pounced on the pitch like a house cat on a roll of wool, sending it into short center field on a line. Two base runners scored, Drew ended up on third, and J. C. slid into second, more for effect than necessity, with a double.

The rally was on and Chad was up. Years of practice and an innate determination made him a tough out. He almost always made contact. His prebatting ritual, adopted from an amalgam of professional antics of his favorite players, drove me crazy. I knew it by heart.

First, the bat, in the early innings a black and gray Easton and in the late innings a blue Rawlings, was ceremoniously taken from the rack. He would swing it gently downward in the on-deck circle, then lightly tap the handle, releasing the red metal donut. His red and black Mizuno glove covered his left hand.

He surveyed the field as he approached the box, and words of encouragement rained from the dugout and stands. He could hear his grandma, high pitched in excitement, over the assorted din of anonymous voices.

"Let's go, Chad! Get a hit! Bring 'em home!"

As is typical of boys his age, Chad went to great lengths to avoid acknowledging her presence. On the field of play it wasn't cool to have a grandma. But he knew she was there.

His left hand, upright like a traffic cop stopping cars, asked the home plate umpire for time as he squared his right foot in the box. A small movement of my hand, motioning forward or backward, positioned him depending on the weight of his bat and the speed of the pitcher. Originally reluctant to follow my orchestration, experience and success convinced him that my placement for him in the box had value. His left foot moved into the box, wiggled into the soft, loose dirt, and his left hand took position on the grip of the black Easton.

"Time in," shouted the umpire.

Hungry, his reward stood on second and third, ribbies, the hitter's staple, awaiting his swing. Another slow curve arced outside and looped chest-high across the plate. Chad swung hard and pulled the first pitch deep down the left-field line, far foul and out of play.

"Oh! Straighten it out, Chad! Bring 'em home!" His mother joined the chorus from inside the concession stand where she cooked red dogs and popped popcorn.

My eyebrows raised. I clapped my hands and said nothing. He knew. I knew. His mom and grandma knew.

Back into the box and the routine. The second pitch was low and harder, and he pulled it foul, too, on the ground past third. Two strikes. He stepped back out of the box. Both base runners had moved back to their bags but were expecting advancement. Chad very rarely struck out.

The third pitch was high but was too close to take. He took it. I winced. The umpire called ball.

"Two strikes, Chad! Nothing close now," I cautioned, a bit upset for not telling him sooner but thankful it hadn't hurt.

The fourth pitch was in the dirt, stopped alertly by the catcher. Ball two.

A walk, I thought, *would be okay too.* Bases full, no outs. It could still be a big inning. He had other thoughts, because you can't convince a young boy that a walk is okay if you can get a hit, and the fifth pitch, which was low and ball three, was fouled off instead. Still 2–2.

The coach called time and came out to talk to his infield. My mind wandered back, back to a game when Chad struck out swinging with the bases full to end the game in defeat, and I faced him and his teammates on the bench. Tears were in his eyes. You wonder if it's right or wrong to put them through all of this, if the ups offset the downs. You ask yourself questions that hurt for an answer. Then instantly, you flash back into the game, never getting one.

A week from now it would be just one pitch in one game, one slow, sly curve, waited on patiently and swung at with precise vengeance. That day, as the ball rainbowed into deep left-center field, rolling to the fence, two base runners waved home, Chad rounded second then slid headfirst and inartfully with a thud into third, beating the throw from center easily. It was a triple. A two ribbie highlight, a triumph, a victory of one boy over another.

He called time as he lay flat, arms cradling third. Then he got up and dusted himself off. To the compliments of his team, he adjusted his hat.

"Nice going, Chad! Nice hit." The screams rose again.

He quickly glanced up into the stands and into the concession stand, from whence the earlier ignored voices came. A mother and grandmother were watching and now less than composed. And in a brief, instantaneous flash of intuition, a quiet smile in his eyes gave me the answer I had sought moments earlier in my wandering memory.

Anticlimactically, the rally fizzled out like a wet firecracker on the Fourth of July, and Emerson picked away at the lead until, in the seventh, the score was a precarious 4–3, Homer leading.

The rules of Little League require that every player participate. The quality of skill possessed by any player is important, but it does not prevent participation. Every player is required by the rules to play at least six defensive outs and bat at least once. It is a good rule. The rule encourages less skilled players to participate and provides the basis of pleasant, unexpected surprises. It affords a learning opportunity to young and old, which might be gladly bypassed by most coaches in order to win. The rule requires participation in each game by that little-used player and affords to that child a chance to prove himself that which is denied him elsewhere. It is a good rule. Except for that day.

Every team has one. He does not field as well; he does not throw as well; he surely does not hit as well as the others. It's the law of nature and Little League. The strong survive; the weak bat last and play right field. The coach, painfully aware of "the rule," inserts him into the lineup where he'll do the least amount of damage. He is hidden, unobserved and unnoticed, in the happy prospect that his play will be completely uneventful, since the coach is convinced that only misfortune can come from his insertion into the lineup. Anticipating the last two innings and smelling a win, the coach massages the lineup hoping that this player's time at bat will come quietly and pass quietly, and that balls hit his way will be fielded by others. The coach takes that boy, whose diminutive skills set him apart ignominiously from the others, and inserts him into the lineup, hoping for anonymity. It is late in the game, it's 4–3, and Emerson gets last bat.

Like other coaches before me, and those who may follow, I stand accused. Accused of careless, inconsiderate insubordination. Baseball, the game that redeems, can likewise be the game that rejects. A coach can subordinate one child's heart to the effort to succeed and in so doing, deny him a chance at redemption. In that, the coach subordinates the innocent desire of one small boy to succeed to the team's obstinate communal desire to win. I stand accused. I plead guilty.

Then, like a drama played out before my eyes and the other eyes of the unbelieving, I was redeemed from my behavior. I was saved not by my own actions but by the simple swing of a bat, by one of "those" kids, who, batting ninth in the top of the seventh and final inning, knocked the cover off my cute deception and taught me a lesson I may not have learned any other way.

Jason wasn't very good. I knew it. The team knew it. The fans knew it. It was not the kind of thing you could keep secret. Silent prayer to the Lord was in order when a ball was hit to him in the field. Against a hard-throwing pitcher my foremost hope was that he wouldn't be hurt. Three pitches, three swings, and sit down. Yet as obvious as it was to anyone with two good eyes, it was equally as obvious that Jason didn't know it. No one told him. He continued to try, continued to swing, continued to play and believe in his own doggedly determined way that he could, indeed, do it.

His dreams were not marred by the skepticism of an adult intellect. In his dreams he hit hard fastballs just as far as other boys did in theirs. His diving catches of sinking line drives were just as spectacular. His dreams of congratulations, of warm welcomes into the dugout by his teammates after a fine play were just as real, just as sweet. Everyone knew Jason wasn't very good, except Jason.

It was still 4–3. It was our last bat, and we needed an insurance run. We would face their 3-4-5 batters in the bottom of the seventh. I had inserted Jason in the lineup not expecting this. We had runners on first and second and two out.

"Jason, you're up," I called out to him as he sat on the bench. His not being ready irritated me, but I said nothing. I called time and went to talk to him. His red and dusty helmet, which he pulled down over his cap, fit poorly.

"Jason, there are two outs. We need you on first. Let's try to get a walk. Watch my signs. Across my chest is take, okay?"

"Okay," he replied.

I walked back to the coach's box at third as he settled into his at-bat stance. I turned, looked down at him, and gave the indicator, a touch to the red bill of my cap then slowly across my chest. He looked down at me, nodded again, and adjusted himself in the box.

The first pitch was a strike. He took it.

"It's okay, Jason. He's gotta throw you another one."

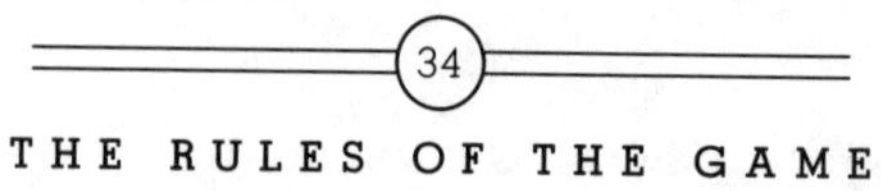

Again I gave him the take sign.

"Strike two!" shouted the umpire after the pitch popped the pud.

I had successfully coached Jason into a 0–2 handicap because I knew the percentages, because I knew the odds. I knew his limitations. But Jason didn't. He backed out again and looked down at me.

"Okay, Jason," I said, swinging my hands together like a hitter shorn of his lumber. "You gotta hit away now. Two strikes." I gave him the hit signal, hoping he would recognize it, resigned to playing defense in a swing.

Jason choked up slightly on that bat–not enough; stepped into the box–too close; and cocked his bat behind his head–too high. The pitcher wound up, and our base runners led off, as much to advance closer to their gloves in the dugout as to lead off base. And then it happened.

Jason got a hit.

A choppy, marvelous, awkward, unexpected, unimaginable, unbelievable hit. It sprayed over the first baseman's head, out of his reach, scooting down the right-field line, barely fair but fair nonetheless, and moved quickly past the right fielder. Two runs scored, and Jason, rounding first like a cul-de-sac, wound up at second, safe.

As he stood at second, I called time and felt, at once, ashamed and proud. Proud for Jason but ashamed that I had given him so little chance to do what he so clearly knew he could do. Ashamed that with all my experience and knowledge, his dreams were still bigger than mine. Ashamed that I had let percentages, averages, and odds, mere pretenders in the statistical show staged with hope and wonder, to nearly take from a young boy a moment I could not in my wildest dreams imagine—a moment he would not in his deepest memory ever forget.

After the third out, Jason's teammates yelled and screamed again as he ran in from second to get his glove and go out to right field. They slapped his back and laughed, and he beamed back at them, at first a sheepish grin then, uncontainable, a full-fledged, toothy "I-did-it-myself" smile.

I honestly can't recall whether we won the game or not. It's been a few years, and somehow it didn't seem all that important. I do recall riding home that night in a yellow school bus over the hills on gravel roads that roll gently between Emerson and Homer. I sat near the front of the bus and listened to the playful postgame banter of boys caught in a moment that would be too soon gone. They talked, as I recall, not about winning or losing, not about their plays. They talked rather about Jason's hit, and he sat there among his friends, quiet, content, happier than he had ever been, and listened to the pleasant sound of acceptance and wished it would never end.

4

TALKING DON'T COOK THE RICE

But far more numerous was the herd of such,
Who think too little and who talk too much.
John Dryden, "Absalom and Achitophel"

This winter I'm working out every day, throwing at a wall. I'm 11–0 against the wall.

Jim Bouton, *Ball Four*

After much thought and deliberate consideration I have come to what for me is an inescapable conclusion about a disturbing trend in our society today. There is too much talk.

We talk about social problems and conference about solving them. We talk about political upheaval and allow the news to shape our views of our lives. We talk about religious revival and the new understanding we have of God's plan for us, then we talk about what we will begin to do about it. We talk about crime, then we pass resolutions that are shaped by the spin on the evening news rather than the real issues we face in our streets and homes. We talk about getting fit, then we talk about the jogging shoes on sale at the local mall. We have allowed talking to substitute for action, and inevitably, as our will to solve any problem or deal with any issue becomes secondary to a new hotter, flashier issue, the talk becomes muted then fades away altogether.

Our national obsession with talk has left us paralyzed and unable to make decisions. When we deal with our children, the same holds true.

Often we adults set out to teach our children in the finest tradition of American education. We start by using methods tried and true—but they turn out to be ultimately ineffective unless underpinned by a strong commitment to do as we say. There is nothing quite so transparent to a child, especially one of Little League age, than an adult giving breathing instructions with his nose plugged. Children, sharp eyed, see quickly through the cloud of hypocrisy. To become effective parents, teachers, coaches, we adults must not only say what we want from our children, we must also do what we say. Only consistent actions will do. Talk won't do it.

The kids who play Little League emulate the best of today's athletes. They dress like the pros, they warm up with the same distinctive rituals, and they even talk like the pros. Kids talk the talk of today's athletes.

We are bombarded by an entire industry that has encouraged athlete-speak. Sports magazines by the score are devoted to what one star says about his team or himself. Television is overwhelmed with meaningless, self-aggrandizing interviews of athletes talking about their ability, their problems, their place in history. Sports clothing manufacturers have developed entire lines of products modeled after the "trash talk" evident at nearly every contest.

During the NBA Eastern Conference finals in 1993, an entire story line was devoted to the various Chicago Bulls players and their New York Knicks counterparts, detailing the nature and significance of their respective trash talk. I found it especially interesting that during the postgame statistical summary not once was anyone given credit for "talking in a three-pointer," "talking down a rebound," or "talking away a steal."

Our national sports press glorifies the athletes experienced in self-promotion. "Colorful," they call them. Yet, inexplicably, more often than not the press avoids the athlete whose accomplishments speak for themselves the eloquent language of achievement. The press avoids an athlete not gifted as a speaker until young boys and girls, untrained in media distinctions, recognize ability and clamor for the person not the persona.

Juan Gonzalez, a gifted and special baseball player who is limited as a home-run hitter only by the constraints of longevity, plays in virtual obscurity for the Texas Rangers, partly because his native tongue is not English. Another former Ranger, Nolan Ryan, a quiet, methodical man of character, was relatively ignored for much of his career until the combination of strikeouts and no-hitters and middle age propelled him into the national spotlight. His story, his character as a man, showed him to be a simple and hardworking team player more comfortable raising cattle than the banner of his own greatness.

We have grown enamored of the sparkle and flash. We have become fixated on the glitter. Our greater sportswriters—Red Barber, Roger Kahn, Robert Creamer, Roger Angel, Jim Murray, and others—manage to see through the hype. Their writing, their words, and their talk detail the simple truths so evident yet so often overlooked in the world of sport.

Unfortunately, they write for an older audience, and the reality of the image shaped for our children usually comes from a twenty-five-inch box, not the written word. We may lament the emulation of athletes by our young, but we must recognize that they will build their foundation of emotional and physical action by tapping into any source that is available. Because of that, it is our obligation, on and off the Little League fields, to instruct with intuition, illustrate by example, correct by conscience, and acknowledge our own failings. It is as much our obligation to offer good example as to shield children from the bad.

Thundershowers had swept down late last evening from the ominous gray-black clouds, an iridescent light show dropping hail and heavy rain across the area fields. This morning the still-drenched ballfield welcomed the sun.

By midsummer, the field had become used to the intermittent rains and shed the water easily into the lush summer grass of the outfield. A spot behind second remained wet, where water drained and stood silently. But the sun and a drag on the field an hour before game time had left the field soft, slightly moist and drying, ideal for baseball.

The baselines were laid in lime. The batter's box and coach's box contrasted sharply against the moist brown dirt. The field, always inviting, almost looked too good to play on, the way a field is supposed to look before the first cleat mars its pristine surface.

As the boys gathered for the game, they approached the field with a curious reverence. To them the field was at the same time too pretty to touch and too alluring to ignore. They teased with their cleats at its edges, down the line but not over it. A half hour to game time they gathered dutifully in the dugout.

Today we played a team from Pender, a village south of Homer, settled in the rolling hills of the Missouri River valley. Their mascot was a dragon. We had played them earlier in the year, and it was our turn to host them. We had beaten them soundly, 10–4, and the experience had left our boys confident, perhaps too much so.

"Hey," said Chad, pointing across the infield. "That's their pitcher. We clubbed 'em last game."

"Yeah, he's weak. I hope he's pitchin' today," added Eric, adjusting his hat and pulling at his pants in a nervous habit that had become a trademark.

"Remember, their catcher can't throw it to second. Be stealing on him." Travis, always alert for an opportunity, had stolen four bases the last time these teams met.

"And hit it to the outfield 'cause none of them can catch a fly," added Drew, on his feet, ready to play.

All of the boys added a fact here, a memory there, recalling the last game, the hits, the opponent's weaknesses, remarking on the ease of prior victory. I felt confident also. We had beaten Pender easily, and we had not played our best game. On this perfect baseball day it looked like short work again. The banter continued as we took the infield, but a few bad throws and misplayed balls scratched an uneasy, jagged line in my placid self-confidence.

I knew my boys. I had coached them for four years and could tell when they were ready to play. Each boy had his own character, his own telltale sign of alertness. Arriving late and eating a candy bar usually signaled Brian had only recently awakened and had missed lunch—red flag. Helter-skelter hustle and a forgotten hat told me Shawn might not be as interested in the ball game as in the trail ride scheduled for tomorrow. A jaunty, confident manner told me J. C. wasn't wearing his game face, a normally brooding visage, hiding elation and disappointment. A lazy meander toward a passed ball told me Chad wasn't prepared to face the rigor of an organized ball game. These signs manifested themselves slowly, never in unison, so it was difficult to gauge the readiness before the game. Usually.

Today, however, the manifestation during the pregame warm-ups and during and after infield practice laid itself before me like a surreal portrait, a panorama gone wrong, a parade of horribles. All talking aside, I could tell that none, not one of the boys, was ready to play today. They had won the game a few weeks ago, and that was enough to win it again today.

I sat on the bench and watched as Pender took infield. Drew was pitching. He and Chad warmed up to the left of the dugout. Three of the boys commenced a burping contest which, under different circumstances, I would have rated as one of the best of the season. Eric won it, of course. My uneasy sense only made it an irritant.

Suddenly I noticed a flash of white to my left, and I saw Drew's warm-up pitch hit the fence of the dugout, three feet over Chad's outstretched glove. I moved silently down the bench, placed a batting helmet on my head, and returned to my seat. I said nothing.

I had learned a lesson a few years back. There are times to actively exhort and motivate players, and there are times when no amount of exhortation will impact them in the least. I was coaching an ice hockey team on which my boy played, in Sioux City, a town not particularly known for its hockey, but one that had developed a fine youth hockey program. It was a house league game where local teams played one another rather than a team from another town. Players of differing ages and skills were grouped together on a team during those games.

We were playing the team with the best house league record, and we were playing miserably. Hockey is a game divided into three periods, and during house league, each period was a ten-minute running clock. It was into the second period, and we were down 8–3, having just given up a weak goal for lack of hustle by our forwards and ineffective play by our defensemen. In hockey you are allowed one time-out during a game, and it is usually saved for an opportune time late in the game to set up a power play or a defensive set to stave off a last-minute offensive desperation flurry. I called it then.

The boys skated over to me on the bench, hot tired gasps of breath sending puffs of smoke out of their face masks in the cold arena. For about ten seconds I said nothing, not so much for effect as for a simple loss of words. These boys were eleven to thirteen years old, tired, probably thinking about their dinners waiting on stove tops at home, and they were all pretty well convinced that this game was out of hand. There were, however, a few older boys on the team who were intensely competitive, and I knew that that was the kindling under which I needed to light the fire if we were to have any chance to get us close, or at least make it respectable. The rest of them were wondering why I had called a time-out, the only likely effect of which would be to delay dinner.

"These guys are not that good." I spoke calmly at first. Their averted eyes turned to me.

"You are playing like a bunch of girls!" Now, I have seen a girls' hockey team from Minnesota play, and they were one of the finest teams around, regularly beating boys their own age, so this remark, intended as an insult, was neither fair nor accurate. Boys at that age, however, are loathe to admit girls can do anything well, therefore the remark seemed to have its intended effect. Still, I did not have them. I was desperate.

"You are embarrassing me!" This got me nowhere, except with my son, who still felt some concern for my feelings.

"You are embarrassing yourselves!" I was really hitting close to home. Boys don't want to look bad to each other, and this remark reminded them of their own abilities and their diminished effort during the preceding period and a half.

I looked around, searching for that one motivating spark to convince this exhausted group of players to do more, to be better, even if for just a moment. My eyes gazed over their helmets and across the ice arena now cut up by the multitude of blades working the once smooth surface. I noticed a small crowd of dedicated fans, a cadre of people cuddling hot chocolate and taking this break from the on-ice action to catch up on the latest news. It hit me like a tax audit.

"And you are embarrassing your mothers." I pointed across the ice, up into the stands. In each boy's mind his eyes met hers, and at that instant, at that special magical moment, a new resolve was born in each of them. They were no longer weary, and dinner would wait.

The mothers could not hear me, but a few saw me point. I wondered what they were thinking as I looked back to the reddish faces of my team.

"Now let's play hockey."

Almost immediately it became apparent that the boys were different. We scored three quick goals to end the period. Before it was over, we scored three more. One came with just a minute left and won the game. These boys were ready to be motivated, and I happened to luck into the only ploy, the only emotive response that could have provoked them into the kind of personal action needed to win the game. I often wondered how motivating to them my comment would have been on a full stomach, but I gave it no further thought. You can move them when they are good and ready.

As I sat on the bench with my team of ballplayers that warm summer afternoon, I realized, reluctantly, that there was nothing I could say that would have one iota of impact on these boys as they waited to take the field. They were all quite full. They had talked themselves into overconfidence and out of any chance to play well enough to win the ball game.

I think it is best to allow young players to learn their own lessons. When something like that happens, I try not to convince them any differently than they have convinced themselves. Some lessons are better learned the hard way; in fact, some can rarely be learned any other way. So as difficult as it was, as opposed as I was to the resigned acceptance of that attitude in a player or a coach, I knew that on this day, the lesson to be learned was probably more important than the game.

Fortunately, there is a ten-run rule in Little League designed to spare one team the agony of the outrageous loss and to allow family and fans to make it home before the ten o'clock news. After five innings and our feeble last at bat in which we fouled out to the catcher, struck out, and popped up weakly to third base, the team, only eighty minutes earlier as confident as a Republican in Orange County, trudged defeated and dejected back to the dugout. Following ritual, we gathered up the equipment and met under the light pole near left field.

"If you want to play baseball and play it well, you have to prepare," I said. "That means practice. If you practice, you become prepared, able to play. But to play you have to come prepared, and practice is left behind on the practice field. Today, you all weren't ready to play. It wasn't that you weren't able to play; you weren't ready to play.

"It's not bad to lose to a team that's better than you. There's no shame in that. And sometimes you'll lose to a team that gets a few breaks or plays outstanding ball, even though they're not better than you. There's no shame in that. But if you come to a game half prepared or, worse yet, unprepared, you beat yourself before you even start. When you don't give yourself a chance to do your best, whether you do your best or not, well, boys, there's something wrong in that. I hope you remember that; I hope that's a lesson that will stick with you. You can talk all you want about how to play the game, but, boys, talking don't cook the rice."

Not much more needed to be said; not much more was said. The boys were bright—most kids that age are unusually perceptive—and they understood what had happened before our talk. They would learn from it. Yet they would make the same mistakes again.

Was there something I should have done? Had I made the same mistake the boys made? Shouldn't I have known better? I had years of life experience, valuable because the lessons learned are etched in the bedrock of human understanding, hard and fast, permanent and enduring, even if changeable.

Yet even the wisest and most experienced will fail on occasion to follow the lessons he has learned. He might drift aimlessly away from the safe path, which experience has taught him to tread. He might detour off the main road to destinations unsafe, new and unknown. Fully expecting the lessons to be learned by the children on such occasions, he comes to the unsettling awareness that his own experiences, far more significant, have not taught him well enough on those occasions to prevent a recurrence of his own mistake.

We pack our bag, pick up our lives, and move on. If tomorrow we face again a mirror reflecting back those errors and mistakes we made, we cannot talk our way back to redemption. If lack of preparation has left us wanting, we must stop and examine our lives. If in the quiet introspection we are found wanting, we should remember as best we can that in life, too, we must come with our actions, not just our words, prepared to play the game.

5

PRACTICE MAKES PERFECT

Multiplication is vexation,
Division is as bad;
The Rule of three doth puzzle me,
And Practice drives me mad.

Anonymous, 1570

There is no homework.

Dan Quisenberry, 1981, Kansas City Royals pitcher, on what was the best thing about baseball

In the farming and ranching country of rural Nebraska, springtime bursts on the plains like a splash of warm water on a cold face—the rolling hills of native grama, the cold, wet, black earth of the Missouri River bottom flatlands. Winter releases its harsh grasp on the countryside, as rivulets of melted snow form at peaks, rushing downward to form larger pools of water in the still-frozen fields. Often, after winter has vacated, it returns again, like a dying leviathan, out of the depths for one last lash—whipping winds, dropping snow, still powerful, yet finally beaten back by the inevitable seasonal change.

As the countryside, like nature itself, arises from the long sleep of winter, the activity of spring, usually in early or mid-April, begins. Huge machines lumber out of the sheds, pulling discs and harrows into the now nearly dry fields, turning up soil, preparing the seedbed for the planters to follow.

On the wet fields of bromegrass, heavy cows drop unsteady new calves, white-faced and uninitiated, soon sucking at the teats of their mothers, routine and automatic. There is a constant symphony of young calves in search of misplaced mothers in wandering herds, diesel machines belching white-black smoke while chugging heavily under the strain of too much to do. The incessant bustle of activity in the farmlands is played out every year.

At the same time the Red Sox and Yankees, the A's and Royals venture to their comfortable southern climes to start spring training, young boys and girls begin to turn their attention from basketball and track to their own annual rebirth, their return to the grasses of Little League. Old gloves are dusted off, struck with a closed fist on an open hand, and reunited with the spirit of renewal. Last year's caps are slapped on a thigh to remove the dust and pronounced fit enough for practice.

In front yards and side streets away from the still-wet fields, in parking lots and driveways, balls are thrown back and forth between solitary children. As they toss baseballs, last year's triumphs are retold and future successes are foretold.

"Dad, where's my glove?" shouted Chad, half-inside the downstairs closet.

"I didn't wear it last. Where did you put it?" I responded, shifting in the chair as I drifted through the Sunday *World Herald*.

"If I knew where I put it, I wouldn't have to ask where it is."

I had seen enough of the paper. Outside, a warm spring day awaited, the buds of the cottonwood trees just beginning to appear. A nip in the air would require a sweatshirt, but the warm sun would soon make it too hot to wear.

"Did you look upstairs in your bedroom?" I asked.

My daughter, Mandi, appeared at the top of the stair rail wearing baseball pants, a sweatshirt too short for her–she'd grown over the winter–and black cleats that I recognized as her brother's from two years ago. This obviously had the mark of a conspiracy plotted by siblings and designed to get me off the chair, out of the house, and throwing a ball.

"Will you play catch with us?" she asked. As I write this, I can think of no sweeter words–now bittersweet in my inability to respond.

"Sure. Let's find the gloves." I went upstairs and after searching unsuccessfully, called in the reserves. My wife found all three and a good, nearly unused baseball in the garage where they had lain abandoned since our last game in August. We went out into the front yard, located some high, dry turf, and began throwing the ball.

We threw three-sided ball; Chad to me, me to Mandi, Mandi to Chad. We warmed our arms, short distances at first, then easing the triangle apexes outward until we were about thirty feet from each other. We threw in gentle arcs to each other, a little gentler to Mandi, as she was new to catching a baseball, more accustomed to a softball. The lazy sun, melting small drifts of snow, radiated off the ground and began to mesmerize me with a rhythmic resonance, nature and man, winter and spring, father and child.

Chad threw with an easy nonchalance that belied a deep competitive spirit; Mandi, with an exuberance that bubbled like boiling water on an unattended stove. We soon lapsed into a game we played together, counting the number of consecutive catches, alternating pop flies with sudden line drives. Chad and Mandi had to work together, yet individual catches were needed to keep the streak alive. One mulligan each was allowed. We got to twenty-seven catches in a row before one of them dropped a fly ball thrown over their shoulder, and the game ended.

We drifted back onto the porch where I sat later, quietly contemplating a small game of catch with two angels of my life. Genetically and geographically joined, a Pythagorean symmetry, beautiful but temporal, too soon gone. I sat there a long time, alone with my thoughts until they too left in the coolness of the waning glow of day, and I got up and went inside.

One of the biggest lies of today, perpetrated primarily on the youth of America—a lie on the same scale as "The check's in the mail" and "I'm from the government, and I'm here to help you"—is "Practice makes perfect." It is not a malevolent lie; in fact, it is a lie which has a basis in experiential fact. But perhaps that is the worst kind. It is used ostensibly to motivate performance, and it has developed a close relative, even more deviant: "Perfect practice makes perfect."

The simple idea behind the lie is that if you develop a practice regimen that does everything as specifically and accurately as possible, the ultimate result is perfection. On that false assumption rest the broken dreams and inexcusable heartache of scores of children who, seeking the unreachable achievement, fail to reach it.

A goal is a good thing if achievable. If the goal is perfection, it is quite clearly unachievable. So practice, or worse yet, perfect practice, designed to make the outcome perfect, is a deception which leads to harmful and unfulfilling expectations in our minds and in the minds of our children.

I did not come easily to this conclusion. Every fiber in my emotional makeup tells me that practice does make perfection, that repetition and routine pave the way for easy excellence in the real-life situation. I have lived a life under that assumption, and I have given my time to the achievement of that goal. But I have come to understand that what I believed is not true, and it is time to dispel the myth. It is time to end the harmful lie and accept an alternative approach that allows each of us to pursue excellence in our own time and within our own limitations.

Baseball practice comes in the spring like the rituals of renewal on the Nebraska prairie. It is as necessary to the ultimate achievement of successful harvest as the careful toiling in the soil. Practice hones skills and develops new ones in children eager to learn and improve. We practice Little League ball with an attitude of education—learning and teaching. We teach situation reactions and essential skills until, hopefully, each skill becomes like an involuntary reflex, automatic, intuitive, and flawless. That, however, is the rub.

We practiced situation ball during each practice after an hour or so of fundamentals. Fundamentals, in baseball vernacular, are fielding ground balls, catching fly balls, hitting, throwing, and running. Nothing very spectacular, but essential like water to a thirsty man. Situation ball is where we pretend we are in certain game situations and encourage the players to think, so that they learn to react to various situations. Kind of like driver's education when the instructor gives you the turn at the wheel but keeps his foot near the brake. You get to learn how to operate the car, but you're not likely to get hurt if you make a mistake.

Situation ball is laborious. It requires the attention of an entire team. Perhaps that is an unrealistic expectation with a group of thirteen-year-olds. But I like that part of practice because, unlike fundamentals which teach you how to play, situation ball teaches you how to think—the Socratic method on a field of dirt. Here more than anywhere else, it is made clear that perfection is unachievable, and yet the search for perfection continues, unabated by that realization.

We were practicing the squeeze play. When executed successfully, it has all the suspense and intrigue of a John Grisham novel. Short, staccato, explosive. Generally used in the late innings of a close ball game, a coach may signal for it when his team needs a run to tie the game or go ahead. It is a risky proposition, and by its very operation it puts your most valuable base runner in danger.

It's set up like this. With one or no outs, you find yourself with a base runner on third. It can be used with two outs at the Little League level, but the execution must be flawless, and you must depend on the defensive team to miscalculate which base to throw to. The object is to advance the base runner from third to home by starting his steal toward home concurrently with the throw of the pitcher. The batter–at the same time actor and impostor–must decoy the pitcher, catcher, and fielders by appearing ready to hit away. At the last instant he turns to bunt, and as the base runner approaches home plate from third, he lays the bunt down toward either first or third, to an unsuspecting infield. Before they can react, the base runner slides safely into home ahead of any throw to the plate. The run scores. This particular variation calls for the base runner to start as soon as he is sure the pitcher is throwing the ball to the plate. A missed signal, a missed bunt, a pop-up, and he is dead in his tracks. Hence the quaint baseball moniker for this play: "suicide squeeze."

We set up a skeleton defense–first, short, third, pitcher, and catcher. A row of prospective batters at the plate would practice the bunt, and a row of prospective runners at third would practice the steal and slide into home. The rows would rotate to the other line after their turn. This drill was a favorite of mine, allowing several different skills to be practiced simultaneously: pitching and catching, fielding a bunt, bunting and running, stealing and sliding. It emphasized alertness and timing. Since the defensive team knew what was coming, the advantage of surprise was eliminated which made the play even more difficult to execute successfully. We practiced the play for about a half hour, rotating fielders so everyone had a chance to play each position and bunt and steal.

If hitting is an art, bunting is a rare masterpiece. It requires stealth, cunning, timing, hand-eye coordination, reaction, and courage. A diminished account of any of these requirements would cause a bunt to be tipped off prematurely, alerting the infielders, or popping up or fouling off the ball, or missing the ball completely, in which case the catcher stood at home, ball in glove, welcoming the doomed base runner with relish.

The base runner also required a special set of skills. Leaving for home too soon allowed the pitcher to throw to third, catching the runner in a rundown. A rundown is a limbo that is designed to embarrass the runner for his miscalculation then run him ragged with short accurate throws, like a rabbit hunted out in the open by hungry dogs.

After practicing the play, it was clear that only the most experienced players could be expected to execute it successfully. "Practice makes perfect" held us hostage to the ideal, but a realistic analysis was that practice made possible, and nothing more. Storing the situation away for future reference, we went on about our business, finishing the practice with a mock game of two innings.

A coach likes to see the fruit of his labors. We had practiced the suicide squeeze again and again, but had not yet had the opportunity to use it in a real game. We waited patiently.

The game was knotted 6–6 in the final inning. Oakland had just batted and scored two runs to tie the game. We had last bat and had the top of our lineup waiting in the on-deck circle. Oakland countered with a new pitcher, fresh and ready, but he looked a bit shaky, maybe inexperienced, in his warm-ups.

Travis led off. His speed gave him an infield single when the shortstop couldn't get the ball out of his glove in time. The next batter, Drew, hit a fly ball to center that was caught. Travis tagged and moved to second just ahead of the throw.

A passed ball put Travis on third with one out. Our next batter, unaccustomed to the new pitcher, fouled off two looping curves and struck out on a called third strike that looked to be low in the strike zone. Two out.

The pitcher ignored the base runner. His delivery allowed Travis to get a great lead off of third. Chad was up. The first pitch was a ball, and Travis scampered back to third. He took the lead given him, and he was almost halfway to home when the ball was called.

The second pitch was called a strike, low but hittable. Chad liked the ball up in the zone, and as he settled out of the box for the next signal the count stood at 1–1. Travis got another huge lead. Then it struck me, an idea whose time had come. The squeeze, the suicide squeeze. We had practiced it. Chad was a contact hitter who felt comfortable bunting, and we had our fastest base runner on third getting a landslide lead.

The situational practice would pay off with a tremendously exciting finish to a well-played game. I would look pretty smart, assuming that the element of surprise would confuse the fielders, who would throw to home instead of first. The leads Travis had gotten had alerted the third baseman, and he had warned the others about the danger on third. I felt safe in assuming they would react as I expected.

I went to my indicator. I looked at Travis and swept my arm. Skin for steal. I went back to my hat bill, squeezed my nose, and threw in a few decoy signals. It was clear from their eyes, a devious glee, that they had both gotten the signal. The bench saw what was up and held its breath, anxious with anticipation.

Chad stepped into the box and waited. He appeared calm, but his heart jumped, and he nervously twitched his left eye, gazing at the pitcher. Travis, careful, watching the pitcher, took two then three steps off of third. He never got a glance, and the pitcher began his windup. Travis took off for home, too early. But the pitcher, still unaware, continued his delivery to home. Chad's job was to lay down a bunt, to put the ball in play, no matter what pitch he got.

The ball shot off the pitcher's hand toward home. Travis was three-fourths home, and it looked like he might beat the ball there! As the ball approached the plate, Chad squared around. The ball was low, too low. He reached out and put the end of the bat on the dropping sphere. Before Chad was out of the box, Travis started his slide into the plate. Chad took off to first.

It looked perfect. The catcher, surprised, could not move without colliding with Travis, now sliding hard into home. The infielders, in shock, were caught unaware. It looked absolutely perfect.

Travis slid safely into home, and Chad ran past the bunt on his way down to first. The surprise worked, and the only player who had a chance at the ball was the first baseman, but neither the pitcher nor the second baseman was covering a prospective throw to first.

The ball, hit off the end of the bat, was spinning clockwise just inside the first-base line.

All of the practice in the world could not have altered what occurred that day, because it was out of our hands. Maybe it hit something along the baseline. Maybe the ball was too tightly wound. Maybe the earth's rotational inertia tilted the world slightly to the first-base line. Whatever the reason, the spinning ball finally stopped just right of the first-base line, silent, like a bad joke in a rough crowd.

"Foul ball!" shouted the umpire.

Chad, who had rounded first, retraced his steps, dejectedly picked up the bat, and stood alone, waiting for the signal. Travis stopped his premature celebration and trotted back to third.

"I had it stole," he pleaded to no one in particular. "If Chad had missed the ball, I'd 'ave been safe."

He was right.

Instead, Chad grounded out to second, we gave up two runs in the extra frame, and could only score one, losing 8–7. The boys were crushed. Not so much because we had lost—they were learning how to take that. But the play that we had set up so often in practice, the great Houdini of a play, had actually worked too well. We didn't lose because of a mistake, and they wondered how that was fair.

Situational baseball taught us the perfect way for the perfect play. The unaccounted for, the unknown, the x factor, had waylaid our perfect play like a sucker punch. We were hurt—the kind of hurt you feel when you can't quite put your finger on the reason why, and it gnaws into the pit of your stomach.

"You can feel bad about that boys, but you played a good game. You've nothin' to be ashamed of."

"If Chad hadn't'a swung, we'd 'a scored," said one.

Chad knew it was true and felt bad.

"But if the pitch was a strike, and Chad didn't lay down the bunt, Travis was out," I countered.

"Man, we practiced that play. It should've worked," added another, bewildered.

"It did work. Everyone did what they were supposed to do. It was well executed." I was searching for an answer. "But we can't control the ball, and we can't control the field. If we ever get a chance to pull it again, I want you to execute it exactly the same way."

We packed up the bats and balls and left, and I was unsure if anyone was convinced. Practice made perfect, but perfect was found wanting. All we could do was the best we could do, and perfection was an unachievable goal. Whether I could find a way to impart that to the boys, and at the same time encourage them that the search for such perfection was still valuable, remained unanswered as we left to go home that night.

Some may argue the finer points, but as for me, I left perfection on the field. I cast it aside like a cheap trick. It had motivated me for years, in my youth and then in my professional life. Finally I realized that its sparkle was tarnished by the unrealistic hopes we placed in it.

Perfection as an ideal is a sham. You cannot control that which at times determines the outcome of the event, no matter how hard you practice, no matter how well you execute. "Practice makes perfect," and "Perfect practice makes perfect" are lies unless you control the elements, the serendipity of occurrence that floats in and out of our lives like the morning mist. For years I believed that it was the outcome that determined success. But all you can really do is your best, and for me, after that day, that would be enough.

6

BALL CAPS AND GLOVES

Friendship is not always the sequel of obligation.
Samuel Johnson

He was not a bad fellow, no worse than most and probably the same, and not a bad ballplayer neither, when they give him a chance, when they laid off him long enough. From here on in I rag nobody.
Mark Harris, *Bang the Drum Slowly*

It was hidden away for years, a dark but good secret, in the crawl space under the kitchen in my parents' house. I was under there, and we were installing a new pipe from the old sandpoint well into the water-softener inside the house. The sandpoint drew water from about twenty-five feet, cold but full of iron, and as the water flowed into the house, it left a film of iron in the pipes that over the years had clogged them like fat inside an artery. They needed to be replaced. I took a flashlight into the cool, dank, and dark space and struggled with wet tools as we managed to install the new pipe. As I slid out on my back, the beam from the light swept across a strewn accumulation of toys, boxes, and papers that had been stored away and forgotten. I spotted it, and the singular importance of the discovery struck me immediately.

I had not worn the glove since I was five or six. It was flat, small, and awkward. Made from real leather, it was still light colored, having held up well to the ravages of time and the dampness of the crawl space. It was my first glove, and I took it to my chest as I slid out from under the floor.

I brushed myself off absentmindedly, all the while holding on to the glove. I sat down, putting the glove half on my hand. It was too small to fit over anything but my fingers. Instinctively I made a fist with my right hand and pounded it into the glove. My first glove, out of shape and out of fashion, still held for me a special fascination.

The baseball glove of a young child is in many ways a friendly extension of the child. It molds itself to the unique shape of the hand. Try on someone else's glove and you will feel an uncomfortable disorientation; it fits no one but its original owner.

The glove must be cared for, oiled, rubbed, and broken in in a laborious process that evolves and really never stops. Each spring, the glove, hard and dry, needs to be reoiled to make it supple again and ready to unite with the hand and make the plays. Once supple and active, the glove protects the child like a shield from hard grounders and high fly balls.

The baseball glove is the friend of the ballplayer. My reacquaintance with my old friend reminded me of games, years ago, played on the fields and churchyards of Lincoln, Nebraska, where I grew up playing ball organized under the name of "Little Chiefs."

It was hard to believe that my glove, now flat and lifeless from years of neglect, could have contributed to my vivid memories of childhood athletics. But those memories were flooding back into my mind like the downstream side of a broken dam.

I could picture myself on a field near my grade school, John J. Pershing Elementary School, a few blocks from my house, playing third base, the hot box, and becoming my idol, Brooks Robinson. His plays and his stops became my stops, and mine became his. In the effervescence of idolatry, of childlike worship of sports heroes, the glory of third base could not have been played better than by Brooks and me. During the Saturday afternoon games, he taught me speed, courage, and reaction. And he taught me the magic of the glove, always the glove, which seemed huge on his hand. My glove seemed huge on mine, at least in my mind's vision of greatness. Now it looked unusually small, almost pathetic. As I examined it closer, I could make out where I had crudely branded my name and the words "Team 5" and "third base" near the strap.

Later that day, I took my glove home and nailed it by its leather strap to the I beam over the entrance to my garage. My children noticed the glove not long after I nailed it up, but they said nothing. I came home one day and found my son and his friend Dan sitting in the shade of the garage, door open, with the glove in their hands. Dan, towheaded, was full of mischief, but none was present as he and Chad sat almost reverently examining the old, small object. I walked in unnoticed and overheard their conversation.

"I told you. I told you it was old," said Chad.

"I didn't know they made gloves like this," replied Dan, scrutinizing the curiosity in his hands.

"See, it's got his name on it."

"Man, how could you catch with it? It's flat." Dan was amazed.

"I don't know. Just don't get it dirty," advised Chad, gently taking it back from his friend. "It's kind of special, I think. It's Dad's first glove."

Yes, I thought, *it is special.* Until then I did not fully realize just why.

A child's glove can be his best friend, yet it is interesting how quickly they can turn on each other. Once, we were in the field, and our pitcher was keeping the ball low to the opposing team's batters, creating a spate of grounders. All had gone well until the fourth inning. Soft bounces, easy rolls, and true lines were easily picked up and fielded by the boys, and calm reassurance lulled them into a soft, innocent sleep.

Then a ball was hit sharply to the third baseman, and he bent over to field it, but the ball, smooth and flat on the ground, skidded over his glove. He stopped, put his gloved hand to his face and looked, actually glared, at it, and then he angrily smacked it with his free fist. I sat on the bench making a mental note to ask him about his reaction. But as events progressed, the mental note would evolve into a fully lit billboard.

The next batter grounded a ball down the first-base line, not quite hard enough for a double play but a sure out. Brian approached the ball, bent over, and began to pick it up, but as he did, it slipped out of his glove. Then as he frantically tried to retrieve it, it slipped out again, as the batter flew safely by at first. Brian got the ball finally, looked around at the lack of options, and tossed the ball back to the pitcher. He stopped and looked at his glove inside and out, upset.

The next batter lifted a ball to short right field, and John, positioned expertly, waited for it until it plopped easily into the webbing and then just as easily out onto the grass. A quick glance at the disappointing glove followed by a harried throw to the cutoff man left the boy safe at second. John stood in right field and stared at the glove.

This not-so-funny comedy of errors continued until the third out opened the intermission between innings. The disconcerted boys ran off the field reluctantly, afraid to face the coach's wrath but still pleased to be out of that miserable inning.

I stopped and gathered them at the outside of the bench.

"I saw you guys looking at your gloves. Is something wrong?" I quizzed.

Some boys glanced at their gloves again and then quickly looked away.

"Hey, if the glove is causing the problem, let's just leave them in the dugout next inning. I don't want these gloves getting in your way. Just throw 'em in the dugout before you go out on defense."

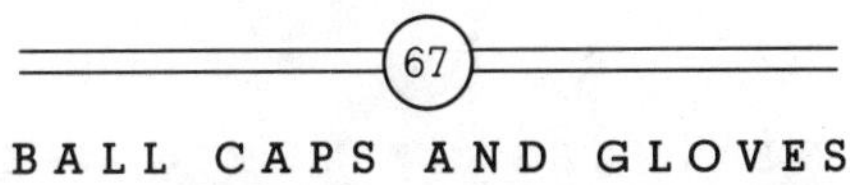

I walked away and sat down on the far end of the bench and read out loud the batting order. One of the boys, who had made an error and who had scrutinized his glove on the field immediately after the miscue, sat down next to me.

"Coach, do you really want us to leave our gloves in the dugout?" He looked up, wondering.

"Sam, if it's the gloves causing the problems, no sense asking for trouble."

He looked, momentarily wrinkled his eyebrows, then smiled a wry smile. At the end of our at bat, each of the boys took his glove, slipped it on his hand, and went back onto the field. I mused about designing a glove that would reflect one's image back like a mirror, so that when a ball was misplayed or dropped and human nature looked for an answer or an excuse, the player would have his answer and would learn the source of his problem.

Friend to the ballplayer, the glove could not be blamed for the faults of the owner nor even for the miscues which had no origin. The boys made the mistakes but didn't blame their gloves again.

The baseball cap, once dull and stoic, has become an imaginative addition to the personality of the child who wears it. An entire industry has recently been built around caps and styles. Walk into any sporting goods store in any shopping mall and you are confronted with a wall, a solid wall of caps.

But it has been my experience that the attachment of a small child to any one of these store-bought hats pales in comparison to the affinity of that child to the hat given him by his own team. There is a mystical, magical bond between boy or girl and team that I came to recognize, though not fully understand, a few years ago.

Homer had always supplied ball caps to its players from T-ball up to Junior Legion. The hats were different colors but inexpensive in bulk. They served their purpose: identify the team and keep the sun out of your eyes. One year, we even used seed corn caps donated by a local farmer who sold seed corn as a sideline to pay for his daughter's college career. All went well, and that was all we knew. Our experience did not open other options.

Then one year, a while back, our community club had the bright idea to upgrade our hats, an idea born in the evening talk after a fish fry that made us feel rich and proud. Buy nice, monogrammed hats for the older boys and girls and make them special, went the talk. We would order special hats, in real team colors and real sizes; no more of this one size fits all. They would bear a team logo "H" in a designer style on the front. This foray into uncharted territory appeared innocent enough, but we were to soon learn that even simple ideas can have unintended consequences.

The hats came one early spring day before school was out. The UPS man delivered them to the local high school because the coordinator was also the high school basketball coach. The caps sat in two boxes unopened for half a day. After fifth period, during study hall, the coach opened them, searched for one his size, and tried one on. The high school colors were red and black with white trim, and the baseball team, though not school-sponsored, had adopted the same color scheme.

The caps were bright red—not fire-engine red, but deeper, truer. The bills were jet black. Over the bill, white and pristine, was embroidered a solitary H in block lettering that stood stark and stylish away from the red background. The bill underside was sewn in green, perfectly stitched by machine, a work of art. Dramatic in its contrast and simplicity, the hat out of the box where it lay with dozens of others was stunning. New, clean, sharp, the hats were an immediate hit. It was a big league event in a little league town.

The boys and girls received their hats and began immediately to put their own imprimaturs on them. My daughter, for instance, is a bender of the brim. She carefully shaped the brim of her hat, molding each side with her small hands, looking in a mirror until they curved perfectly downward alongside her temples. My son shaped his to meet his own self-portrait of who he would become, a mask of his own idol. He put his number in black marker under the bill, where in the weeks ahead a jagged sweat line would ease out to and then past the number, smudging its articulated edging.

J. C., wearing the hat low, shifted it forward on his forehead until he could glare menacingly from under the bill, at least as menacingly as a thirteen-year-old could glare. Dan bent his bill forward yet wore his hat higher on his head. A blond shock of hair hung out from under his bill, and his bright mischief glowed openly from under its shade.

By the end of the day, the hats, once lined up in unison, row upon row of conformity and sameness, now took unique shapes on each unique head. No two hats looked alike, but all were worn with the pride that belonging to a team brings to a young child. Only two rules applied: You lose your hat, you pay for the next one, and you wear it to every game or you don't play.

You might expect the hats to be put away after a few days and then brought out again for practice. These hats did not get put away. They were worn daily, everywhere, by the kids. I saw one embarrassed mother remove her son's hat as he entered Sunday service. Hats bobbed up and down in the crowd at the final spring track meet. Young heads wore them like a red badge of courage, proud and arrogant. The high school parking lot, the local convenience store, the shopping mall in Sioux City, all proved a ready ground for the display.

I was not quite sure why the hats caused such a stir, such a reaction among the players who wore them. At first I thought it was the kind of reaction that came with newness and would soon pass. When that didn't happen, I listened closely and watched as the children caressed, shaped, dusted, and cared for their hats.

Before, my son's hat had been thrown on the bedroom floor, but now this new one was regularly hung up in his room. Before, boys would grab any hat at the close of an at bat. Now they would only don their own hats, searching for them in the dugout, resistant to taking the field without them. Before, I saw the players wearing the hats of their favorite pro or college team, but now rarely did I see any of the boys wearing anything but the red and black caps they took as their own. It was a phenomenon I did not understand.

"You guys like your ball caps?" I asked one day, exploring for an answer as we finished up a practice and put the equipment in the bag.

"Yeah, they're neat," said Ryan, taking the cap off his head and looking at it once again.

"What do you like about them?" I asked no one in particular.

"The colors." "It's fitted." "The *H*." I still was not satisfied. I turned to Jason, who was always wearing his.

"Jason, I bet you sleep in your hat," I joked.

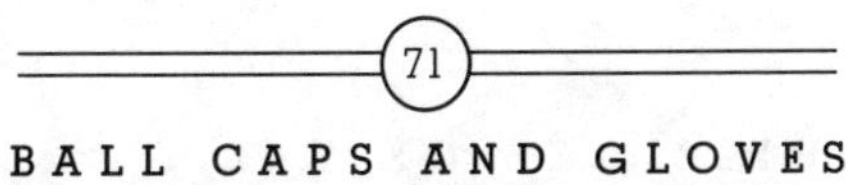

He laughed uneasily, and his slight, embarrassed grin led me to believe that I was closer to the truth than I had expected.

"Nah," he answered and laughed again.

I hadn't gotten any closer to an answer, and I let it drop as the boys moved away. Maybe it wasn't that important, but I pursued it as Chad and I drove home.

"The guys really seem to like their hats," I said, almost a question.

"Yeah." This wasn't going to be easy.

"How come?"

"I don't know."

"I mean, really, what's so great about these hats anyway?" I was searching, persistent.

He took his hat off his head, glanced at the sweat line as he wiped his forehead with his sleeve, and sat the hat loosely on his lap.

"I don't know, Dad." He placed it back on his head, positioning it again, adjusting the bill with a back to front sweep. "I guess we like 'em 'cause they're ours."

All the same yet distinctive. Part of a team yet still an individual. Shaped by their heads, their hands, worn to fit their personalities. Like the glove, the hat became for the boys a friend that always stood with them. The gifts these items give young children learning the game are not easily discovered and may lay dormant for years.

Like so many times in our lives, we slide along, uneasily aware that there is a lesson in what we do. We search vainly for what that lesson is until it is revealed to us, illuminating and enriching our existence. In the small things we can discover the richness of character and take that into our own selves, layer on layer, creating that which did not exist before from that which was always there.

ON WINNING

Not the victory, but the action,
Not the goal, but the game,
In the deed the glory.

Inscription on Memorial Stadium, Lincoln, Nebraska

If I were playing third base and my mother were rounding third with the run that was going to beat us, I'd trip her. Oh, I'd pick her up and brush her off and say, "Sorry, Mom, but nobody beats me."

Leo Durocher

An argument has been raging across our country about the American attitude toward victory, toward winning. In sport, where the object of the game, perhaps on occasion even its sole purpose, is winning, the argument has become an unholy sacrilege to some, a battle cry to others: "If winning isn't important, why do they keep score?" Some of our greatest and most endearing sports heroes are often quoted about their attitudes regarding winning.

This is not to say that winning is overrated. Far from it. I prefer winning to the alternative, much as I prefer pleasure to pain. But pleasure is immeasurable and ultimately meaningless without an opposite sensation against which to measure it. Constant pleasure mummifies the mind and dulls the senses. It is not the win that propels upward the sensitive emotions of young ballplayers but the sense of achievement in the attempt at success.

So a fine line must be carefully drawn, first with a clear understanding of the purpose that winning serves for any particular ball team, and second, with a clearer understanding of the purpose that winning serves for any particular ballplayer. They are often not the same.

We have all seen the epochal sport photo of a team in triumph while another team lies prostrate in defeat at its feet. Joe Namath, one index finger extended, being led off the field after the Jets' remarkable Super Bowl triumph in 1967. Kirk Gibson's hobbled jaunt around the bases after his improbable homer in the last inning for the Los Angeles Dodgers. Michael Jordan hugging the NBA championship trophy, kissing it in tears after his first of three championships. The cameras seem fixated on victory. Then just as quickly the interviewers and cameras switch to the losers' locker room, a mausoleum of mere mortals, to give sympathetic condolence to the defeated.

A few years back, at the end of the Nebraska high school boys state basketball tournament, held in mid-March, a picture appeared in the Sunday newspaper, a picture of a player lying on his back at midcourt, his hands cupped to his eyes. I could not tell whether his team had won or lost, whether his emotion was elation or despair. Only the caption gave away the mystery. The line is that fine.

The humid summer breeze wafted heavily over the raised hilltop field in Blair. The main field where tonight's game would be played was being manicured by a passel of volunteers, raking, dragging, wetting the base paths and relining them with studied artistry. Little League district championships had been decided on that field for a decade, and today would be no different.

Blair, the home team, winners in five of the last eight years, would host an amalgam of Little Leaguers representing different teams from northeast Nebraska. They had been assembled as a unit to compete for the privilege of representing District Three in the state Little League tourney to be held in late July. Our boys warmed up on a nearby field.

This field, named for volunteers and benefactors, was a jewel in the town's array. An outfield fence, dark green, stood six feet high, semiarced around the outfield.

Local merchants, having bought advertising to support the field operation and maintenance, had their business ads neatly painted against the green hardboard background. A home run, rare but reachable, over any particular merchant's ad entitled the player to a gift certificate from the merchant to a local eatery.

A light green carpet stretched from the fence to the infield, a dreamlike blanket. No grass was that green, no yard was that perfect. The base paths were bare earth, yet clean and smooth. The diamond shape contrasted harshly with the infield, as the grass on the first and third baselines was cut like a straight edge toward the opposing benches. A fine mesh gravel, chalky white, mined from the surrounding bluffs near Fort Calhoun, formed a path from each bench to the on-deck circle and then to the batter's box, a runway for the boys approaching the terminal.

Each on-deck circle was a hand-painted rubber cutout, lettered in a colorful "Welcome to Blair, Nebraska" and "Home of Little League District Championship." Each dugout was covered with a roof, and a hard plastic bench sat at ground level. There was enough room for team and coaches, and a younger brother or two if they could sneak in and watch. Roomy and comfortable, it provided the best view of the playing surface.

Behind the benches, toward home plate, three sets of bleachers rose upward, forming an angled U. Higher, above the middle section, sat the announcer's and scorer's box. Below, under the stands to the rear, were the concessions, and an aroma of hot and Polish dogs, popcorn, cheese, and chili circled from behind the bleachers into the stands, beckoning buyers below.

The tournament was double elimination until the championship game, which was winner take all. We had won our first game easily, 11–1, but we played poorly the next night, losing 6–2. We struggled back through the loser's bracket, and last night we had won a tough contest, 5–3. Blair had swept convincingly through the winner's bracket, winning all three games by a combined score of 28–6, and they had sat through last night's game as spectators to see who they would face for the championship. They were rested and confident. Tonight's game would send a team on to the state play-offs. Just before game time the lights were turned on, too early to appreciably be noted at ground level.

The national anthem was played to the crowd on a record player, and I felt cheated. I was soon buoyed by a rare treat. A young boy, the brother of one of our players, suffering from a disease which kept him smaller than his heart allowed, sang with great bravado and spunk, "Take Me out to the Ball Game." Harry Carey would have been proud. Although Blair was the home team, this being their field, we won the flip and elected to bat last. Our boys took to the field.

In order to advance to the championship game, last night we had been forced to use our best pitcher, Alan, a whip of a boy who threw alternately smoke and pasta. Little League rules prevented his pitching again tonight. We knew that with a day off, Blair would be throwing their best at us. Our hope was to stay close and get lucky in the late innings. You make your own luck.

The first three innings were routine. Bret, pitching for us, was workmanlike, accurate but not overpowering. He couldn't put together three straight outs and as a result, we had given up a run in each inning. He had recovered each time to strike the next batter out; he was pitching well. Of our first nine batters, five had not touched a pitch. But all of the boys had had a look at their fireballer, which was encouraging. The second time around should be easier. The game, scheduled to go six innings, was half over, and we trailed 3–0.

Blair was batting in the top of the fourth. The night by now had fully enveloped the field, held in check only by the illumination of the surrounding light poles. The air, slightly less humid now, had begun to settle heavily around us, and a faint breeze blew in from the west. Buzzing gnats and mosquitoes and night things flew aimlessly above our heads, close to the lights, washing in and out of illumination, a cloud in the vastness of the dark night sky.

Bret was tired. He walked the first batter on five pitches and looked to be overthrowing, a condition in which the mind tells the body to compensate for a satiated spirit. The next batter hit him hard into right field, but the fielder played it nicely, holding him to a single. With a man on third and first, it looked like a steal coming. Down 3–0, every run was crucial. The team was being coached by committee, several of us assisting, put together as coaches for the tournament. Bret was my pitcher, so I made the trip to the mound.

"Hey, Bret, how's the wing?"

"I'm okay." He shook his head. He was the kind of boy who would tell you if he weren't, even if just with his eyes.

"They're going to send the base runner on first on your first pitch. We want the runner on third if we can get him."

Chad, catching again, had come to the mound with me.

"He's taking a big lead on third, trying to get your attention, Bret," Chad offered.

I looked at no one in particular, trying not to give anything away.

"We'll give 'em second," I said. "Bret, look over to first a few times, try to make them think you'll throw over there. Pitch a fastball on the outside. Chad, if you catch him sleeping at third, take him."

Chad smiled slightly, nodded to Bret, and put the ball into Bret's glove. I had seen that smile before. It was the devious smile of a young boy in control of a big surprise.

Bret went into a stretch, looking to first, then home, then to first again. The base runner on first danced on the balls of his feet, back and forth on a string between first and second. The base runner on third, clapping his hands, exaggerating his presence, had a huge lead but was going nowhere.

In the dugout I spoke without moving my lips like Edgar Bergen. "We're gonna nail him at third."

The bench and the other coaches glanced at his lead, looked back to me, and waited. The edges of Chad's eyes behind the red metal mask flitted left to third, then back to Bret. A solitary index finger held next to his thigh signaled the pitch.

As soon as the windup started, the base runner at first took off. The first baseman and I yelled almost in unison.

"Chad, he's going to second!"

The batter was taking it all the way, and the ball hit the catcher's mitt with a thud, strike on the outside corner. All eyes, except Chad's, were on the base runner nearing second. The runner at third, delighted in doing his distraction, turned spectator and watched momentarily.

Chad pounced ahead, eased by the outside throw, and cocked the ball, unhesitatingly, and fired to third. The base runner, caught

unawares, stumbled slightly, then desperately struggled back toward the base. Dan waited at third, having been alerted by Chad through some signal of which I was unaware. Dan's glove was next to the bag and ready for the ball. The runner at second slid safely into the bag, but the real play at third was out easily as the tag was slapped on the runner's left forearm that never even reached the bag. The stumble helped, but you make your own luck.

Bret, invigorated with the adrenaline of surprise, settled down quickly and struck out the next two batters. We were still in it.

As I looked at the scorebook in the bottom of the fourth, I reminded the players that Blair's pitcher was throwing a no-hitter. It may be superstitious bad luck to remind your own pitcher of that, but I think it is mandatory motivation to remind your team when one is being tossed against you.

Our first two batters, singularly unresponsive, struck out. Then Chad broke up the no-hitter with a single to right field, and Dan followed with a long hit to right field pulled by his smooth left-handed swing. Chad rounded third, scoring ahead of the throw. A spate of hits and walks followed, and before the third out was registered, the game was tied at 3–3. Better yet, their ace, upset and angry, was pulled after the third run. He was gone for the night, and our hopes heightened.

The next two innings saw each team space a hit around a walk and a solid defensive play, and the lead seesawed each half inning. At the end of five it was 5–5. Three great defensive plays in the top of the sixth kept the bases clean, still 5–5, with our at bat coming up.

Our lineup had changed as substitutes were inserted, but it should have made little difference, being a team of all-stars. Our first two batters, however, hit weak ground balls at ready fielders, and it looked like extra innings.

John, up next, reached on an outfield error, a misplay in the night lights. A walk moved him to second, and he went to third on an infield single created when the shortstop hesitated, thinking lead runner first, then remembering he had two outs, threw lamely and late to first. Two outs, tie game, bases full. Chris was up.

Chris was not much of a hitter, but he had the eye of an art critic. He walked more than he hit. Nerves of steel. To him, not taking a close one meant don't swing at balls. He rarely guessed wrong.

The first pitch looked good, and it was. Chris took it for a strike. The bat didn't move off his shoulder. The second pitch was wide, called a ball, and nearly got away from the catcher. John looked in from third but stayed put. The third pitch was low, called low, and Chris stepped back out of the box—2–1.

The pitcher looked to be struggling. He was aware, I felt, that a walk meant the ball game. He was tight as new spandex. The next pitch, aimed not thrown, was inside. 3–1. Chris got a take sign, but he didn't need it. Unless the ball was perfect, he wasn't swinging. It was. He didn't. 3–2. Full count. Bases full. Big game. I felt ill.

The pitcher waited, nervous, weak. He had no place to hide. He wound up and threw the ball. Chris never budged his bat. The ball was wide, and Chris knew it.

"Strike threeeeee!" shouted the umpire.

Chris was surprised, genuinely surprised. You can usually tell if a player thinks an umpire is wrong or is just covering up his own failing by pretending to think the umpire was mistaken. Chris came back, dejected, the rally dead.

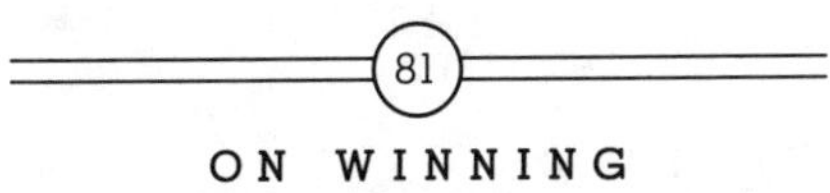

"Where was it?" I asked.

He looked puzzled.

"The pitch?"

"Outside. Way outside." He was right, but you can't play the game and call it too.

We played another two innings, still tied, until Blair edged a run and then another in the top of the eighth. We fought back, managed one run, but Dan flew out to deep left with a player on, which ended the game and our run at the championship. It was, quite simply, the best Little League game I'd ever seen played. The players from both teams received a warm and sustained ovation from the fans as they met at midfield to shake hands.

The boys were down but not dejected. They had faced the best Blair had to offer, struggled against a superior pitcher, knocking him out, and had fought back three times to tie the game when failing to do so would have been fatal. They had played cleanly, fairly, and well. There were few errors and plenty of sharp, well-hit balls.

Chris complained briefly about the called third strike. Then he said that he probably ought to have swung at the two pitches right down the pipe; he was more concerned with his own failing than that of the umpire. Parents, fans, and friends came up after the game and commented that the game was the best they'd seen this year, or any year, and the boys, still smarting, stood around, kicked the dirt, and listened.

I lingered on the field until the lights were turned off. The vapor lamps glowed eerily for a few moments after the power was cut, then they faded to black. I packed up some gear and began walking back to my car with Chad. His sister and mother joined us from the stands. Boys and parents passed us from both teams, and noticing his jersey, complimented his sad face.

"Thanks," he muttered.

We had lost. We had lost what was up to this point in Chad's life the biggest game he had ever played in. We had lost, despite his catching, his hit to break up the no-hitter and start the key rally, and his run-scoring hit to end our drought. He had played as well as he could play on that warm July night, and we had lost.

His mom tried to console him, even his sister, but he hung his head. I asked for his glove and put it underneath my arm as we walked, silently, side by side. I put my right arm around his shoulder. In a few years, I wouldn't be able to do that, but that night, that night I knew exactly how he felt. I knew that there was nothing I or anyone else could say that would help him. I knew that he had done his best, and tonight he had known that it was not enough. And I knew that for the rest of his life, when he looked back on this night, and he would many times, when he looked back on this game and this loss, when he searched deep back into his own memory of his first championship Little League game on that manicured field on a hilltop in Nebraska, he would feel good about what he had done, and he would smile.

8

PITCHERS AND CATCHERS

Not to go back, is somewhere to advance,
And men must walk at least before they advance.

Alexander Pope

Son, what kind of pitch would you like to miss?

Dizzy Dean,
to a batter he'd struck out all day

Baseball is a team sport but allows, even forces, within each game individual head-to-head competition unlike any other sport. The truest form of that naked competition is the battle between pitcher and batter.

I'd read that, or a variation of it, somewhere, and I had accepted it as the gospel truth until I began to watch my son catch. I scrutinized his behind-the-plate activity as he signaled for a certain pitch, accepted it, and calmly directed the pitcher up and down the scale of emotions during each at bat in each inning.

The catcher gives the sign. The pitcher nods, then nods again, like one of those toy poodles found in the rear window of brightly painted vintage Fords. The catcher slightly shifts his posture, inside or out, signaling the placement of the ball, or at least at this level, a hopeful direction of throw. The tit-for-tat orchestration between pitcher and catcher, alternately maestro and accompaniment, modifies the pitcher versus batter battle. It is not simply mano a mano. On any good team it had better be two against one.

The catcher and pitcher work together, and when they are most successful they begin to think alike, not identically, but alike. They begin to comprehend situations similarly, recognizing batters and prospective pitches in an uncanny, seerlike quality. Just as the catcher is getting ready to signal a curve, the pitcher thinks, *I'll throw him a curve; he swung like a boy chopping buttonweed in a bean field last time,* and the two minds click into one cohesive course of action.

The synchronized soul mates, on a good evening, can predict each other's thoughts, not like déjà vu, because there are no reminiscent feelings here. There are no feelings of having thrown the pitch before, but of having picked just the right pitch at just the right time. It's a feeling one cannot have alone.

I suppose you could argue that once the ball is released, it's pitcher against batter, and nothing more or less. That begs the question, for this is not batting practice, but baseball. The pitcher does not face the batter alone—he faces the batter with a catcher, who sits behind the batter, free to do his mischief unseen, yet omnipresent, like an agent for the IRS.

Throughout the storied history of baseball, great pitchers have made good catchers better, and great catchers have extended the weary arms of tired pitchers. Who would seriously argue that Johnny Bench did not contribute significantly to the success of his pitchers throughout his career? While not as accentuated, it is the same in Little League.

Pitching in Little League is like singing solo in a school choir; there are plenty of other voices around you, but you know that when your solo comes, yours is the only voice anyone will hear singing. Pitching is the closest thing there is in baseball to nakedness. A catcher can help you find your pants, but he can't be your belt. It takes a special disposition to pitch and pitch well.

A pitcher has to be a little angry at all times. I've tried with spotted success to make pitchers of boys who simply couldn't get mad. Dan, funny and disarmingly good-natured, could throw the ball with the best of them. Put him up against a batter and he began to lob the ball like an egg. He didn't want to hit a batter. His warm-ups were the best pitches he threw. Rock, on the other hand, wearing a perpetual scowl that burnt too deep, threw one speed:

hostile. He scared every mother and father in the stands. Too angry. I put him in the outfield where his anger could go generally unchallenged and unnoticed.

I do not mean to suggest you should encourage a child pitcher to become unfeeling and insensitive to the batter he faces. He should on no account intentionally throw at another boy. In fact, I discourage trying to teach any Little League player to hurt another or even how to be angry enough to pitch. It can't be done.

You can, however, find a little anger in anyone. The secret is to channel and direct it positively, increase the innate desire to challenge the batter. If a boy does not want to pitch, he can't, but not every boy who wants to can.

It works this way: Anger must be directed at the right time toward the right end. Anger itself is like a blanket, covering everything within distance without discrimination, and therefore it is overinclusive, injuring both good and bad. A pitcher needs focus–he needs to spiral his energy into the pitch and past the batter.

Alan, who had pitched with the all-stars in Blair, was pitching against us one very forgettable summer afternoon. The heat and wind blew in from the southwest, parching the already dry and dusty field. Gusts whipped up mini wind twists, which circled the field, picked up last night's popcorn sacks and napkins, and shuffled them around like playing cards. Players turned their backs to the wind and dust, letting it pass while play was halted.

Alan was a thin afterthought of a boy. He would stand on the mound as the wind blew, almost tottering backward at times. Steadying himself, he looked in for the sign, then thinly and sharply, like a bullwhip, fired the ball into the pud. He worked quickly, in a hurry, throwing the ball, receiving it again, then almost before the batter was ready, throwing again. He wasn't "quick pitching" just pitching quickly, hungry for success, feeding on outs. I thought he'd be full by now. He had mowed down seven batters in a row. Unfortunately his appetite was insatiable.

He was methodical, dispatching our batters like terse telegrams. He was not overjoyed, but a sly smile creased his lips at each out. Alan was enjoying this domination of our hitters. He mixed his pitches. First a low, hard slider. Then, once the batter had that pitch timed, he would throw a nasty, sinful curve, and delight as it evilly twisted our batters out of shape, like wine screws into cork. Our boys, frustrated, out of balance, stomped back to our dugout.

We stayed close only because their bats were as ineffective as ours. We kept their runners off the bases, and it looked like the game might go on forever. There is a time limit in Little League, but that would be no problem. We had played five innings in forty minutes. Neither team had scratched the base at first.

I could have troubled my players with another talk on hitting, but I thought better of the idea. Alan's language was far more eloquent than mine. He seemed stronger at the end of each inning. He was spinning a tapestry, beautiful, a work of art in green, brown, and ball, and I caught myself watching, admiring more than coaching. In the end, they squeezed a run across, and Alan shut us down, striking out the side in the bottom of the extra frame. I congratulated him on his performance, and only then did he break into an open, warm smile. He still shook hands like a man looking for change.

I saw Alan pitch two more times that year, and he was equally effective each time. Off the mound, the kid was quiet, pleasant, polite. On it, he had that angry demeanor, the internal push to be better than the batter. I do not know where it came from, but I could tell it was something that could not be taught. It was ever present internally, hidden yet explosive on demand. Just as quickly it subsided back into the darkness of the young boy's mind. It made for a tough pitcher, but in a way it left me wondering at the reasons why.

Catchers, on the other hand, need to be altogether different. Catching is grungy, dirty, hot, sweaty, and painful work. An angry catcher is useless to his task. Oh, he has reason to be angry, but no outlet for it.

His job, after putting on a hot, wet, and dirty chest protector, shin pads, and mask, is simply to stop any and all pitches, no matter where they're placed. Any part of his body must be willing to gladly take a bump or a bruise to knock the ball down. Then he must accurately toss the ball back to his pitcher. That can't be done in anger. The catcher is the Joan of Arc of baseball, silently suffering indignity, plodding back again and again for more.

My son Chad is a catcher–and likes it. Of course, he is also a hockey goalie, and that says something. He won't admit he likes it. At thirteen, to admit you like something is to risk losing it, so a grudging acceptance is what I'd call it.

I have asked him what it is exactly that he likes about catching, and I have come to a singular conclusion: He gets to be involved in every single play. Even a pitcher can't say that, likely under Little League rules to be removed before a complete game. The catcher gets to call for the ball on every play. He doesn't have to wait and worry that a ball might be hit to him, like those less fortunate in the infield and outfield. He knows that on every play he must be ready, active, agile, reacting to all events that play out before him. A catcher must have a persistent, dogged determination to be in the game at all times—not an easy task in a game that is designed to float lazily between outs, at bats, and innings. An outfielder can spend a moment examining the caterpillar approaching his cleats, and an infielder can lapse into a game of self-indulgent tick-tack-toe with his foot in the dirt. A catcher cannot.

A catcher must be prepared, like a boy scout, only more so. His job is to be a bulwark, the Maginot Line of defense between home plate and a passed ball. He must stop everything using every resource at his disposal, employing his skill and cunning. Ready to pounce and throw a ball to any base, he must be agile and catlike, yet similarly ready to block home base from an approaching runner on third, bull-like and stubborn.

Here's the question: Can you teach these traits, or must you find the right kind of boy to play these unique, idiosyncratic positions? Coaches, legions of them, will argue that foot speed, arm strength, and positioning can all be taught and honed with practice. They say that pitching can be learned with years of experience and work. I would not disagree. Yet I continue to maintain that there is something intangible and necessary to play either of these positions that can neither be taught nor programmed with drills. You can't get soap out of a hoe handle.

This does not mean that you should line up all the five-year-olds on your teams and decide which of them have the tools and makeup to be pitchers and catchers. Frankly, that is done too often too soon, and usually with harmful results.

My suggestion is to let all the boys pitch; let everyone catch early on in their baseball experience. Watch them. If they have fun, let them continue. Encourage opportunity. Request persistence. In time, they'll make your decision easy because they'll let you know if they can do what they must do to pitch and catch by their actions on and off the field.

And before you mark that decision down in indelible ink, try them again. Listen to them. Find out if they're playing ball because they enjoy it. Don't count mistakes or miscues; they'll become too important soon enough. Count the smiles, the enthused responses, the excited yelps of personal success. They are what matter early on. They are the harbingers of a lifelong joy of playing ball. They are the sounds that you will hear after the evening glow and summer warmth have slid away into the fog and mist of an early fall. They are the sounds that resuscitate the lifeless body of a barren winter dream, breathing new life each spring into a new dream, seeking existence and purpose on the soon green fields of Little League.

9

FATHERS AND SONS

Let us show the world at large that the progress of the past few years has reached us too and that today, the word "father" designates not merely the man who has begotten you, but rather the man who has both begotten you and then deserved your love.

Fyodor Dostoyevsky, *The Brothers Karamazov*

Baseball gives every American boy a chance to excel, not just to be as good as someone else but to be better than someone else. This is the nature of man and the name of the game.

Ted Williams, quoted in *Sports Illustrated*

Were I a mother, this chapter might be titled differently, and it surely would not read the same. By illuminating the father-son relationship, I do not suggest any others are less significant or less important. Mothers and daughters, fathers and daughters, mothers and sons—it is not the genealogy that charts the course, as all of these relationships are in their own way vital and valuable. It is rather from a personal intimacy with which I am most familiar, about which I feel compelled to discuss, that I have limited my topic herein. No slight is intended—I hope none is taken.

Between the full panoply of emotion from hate to love, discouragement to encouragement, compassion to indifference, rests an uneasy alliance of father and son. There is no reason to believe that it has ever been different or will ever change. It is immutably that way, has been always, and will always be. But it is a relationship of hope. I once read an opinion editorial written by a black man lamenting the condition of the young men of his race. He said, and I believe the comment applies to all of us, that the best thing a man could do was be a father to his son.

I would add that one of the simplest and best ways to be a father to a son is through baseball. Not the art of baseball, not the competition of baseball, not even the history of baseball, though all are instructive. Rather, through the connection created with a game of catch. Baseball becomes an experience shared, an emotional cartilage that both binds and cushions, wrapping together, inextricably, two men hurtling down a track soon divided by design or destiny.

I can recall playing ball with my father only once or twice. For most of my childhood he traveled hard across the great plains selling farm machinery.

The late 1960s were halcyon days in the short-line machinery business, before fewer but larger farms required bigger but less equipment. My dad was a regional manager, traveling by car over the highways and interstates, which were then still new and unusual, of Nebraska, Kansas, Oklahoma, Iowa, Texas, and Colorado. In the years before his retirement, he drove a brown Chevy Impala, loaded. I liked the car, driving it on my school permit to football and basketball games. Hundreds of miles a day my dad drove, five or six days a week. That left little time for catch. I played mostly with brothers and friends, opting for a vicarious game versus none at all.

But I remember one game of catch with my dad years ago, before we moved to the farm, when we were still living in Lincoln. Two pin oaks, tall and pyramidal, grew like sentinels on either side of the driveway. They were turning into a chlorophyll kaleidoscope of colors, hastened by warm days and cool nights. The resplendent bluegrass stretched from the sidewalk toward the house, losing its way under the bushy evergreens that grew up under the eaves.

Our conversations are now vague. I recall little of what was said, only that I found myself in the shade of the oak throwing a ball to my dad, near the juniper hedge. Back and forth the ball traveled, dim in the shade, then suddenly bright white into the sun and his glove, then back again, white and brilliant, and back into the shade, darkly into my glove. I do not recall how long we played, or why, only that it seemed like forever and ended too soon. I would miss a catch or overthrow him, and I would carelessly chase it into the city street—like a dog after a car tire—while he yelled to be careful. I never thought of being careful. It was not time for care; I was carefree. Not a time of worry but of wonderment. In the endless light of fall, which colored the branches with shifting shades of dark and light onto the yard below, I stood, invincible, playing catch, knowing all was right with my world.

As you grow older and become what you beheld, you seek to recapture the memories with new experiences, new games of catch. On a wall in our home hung a picture of my son, barely able to sit up, with a ball in his hand. "All-star" it said on his shirt. Before he could walk, he could catch. We'd sit cross-legged on the carpet, close to each other, and toss a cloth ball underhand to each other. He clapped his hands together, missing the ball as it dropped in his lap time and again, until eventually he coordinated the clap into a bona fide legitimate catch. I was exultant. And why not? He was catching the balls I could have caught.

We grew up playing catch, playing ball. Chad and I. Other sports occupied the off-season, interlopers on a calendar designed around April to August. Baseball was king; all else was secondary.

I coached ball mainly to spend time with my kids, since my job and profession ate up much of my extra life. I could commit to a practice or a game and schedule it like a court hearing, ensuring my presence, but not otherwise. So on my calendar they went, blocks of time cut out of days allocated to fatherhood.

We would spend a few scraped-together minutes before dinner in a quick game of catch before a trip out of town, barely enough to work up a sweat. But the theft of time became less regular. My schedule offered reprise, however limited, and time to play. It is sad in retrospect–my own life compartmentalized to include "1. Time for my son," like a shopping list of obligations, too many and too narrowly executed to achieve anything approaching significance. I became what I beheld.

One cold winter evening, as a fire I had started in the afternoon embered out in the ashy glow of the fireplace, Chad came downstairs with his catcher's mitt. It was no ordinary mitt, and he had begged me to buy it for weeks. It was expensive, and I balked, finally relenting after he agreed to care for it unlike an ordinary glove. We had bought glove oil for it and had worked it into the fresh, pungent leather with our hands, mine teaching his how. Now, a year later, he was sitting alone on the hearth, glove and glove oil in hand.

"I'm gonna oil my pud. Can I?" He looked up, seeking approval with his eyes, holding the oil in his hand.

"It will just go to waste. It'll dry out before you get to use it," I answered, always the practical.

He looked at me and my comfortable position in front of the fireplace.

"I kinda thought we could, ya know, play catch."

There it was, the motive. Kids are great at acting like adults. The dodge, then the real motive. I looked over my shoulder and out past a double door that led to the side yard. It had snowed last night, and the wind outside, though not violent, still shifted the dry white powder around in a haphazard arrangement.

"Chad, look at it." I pointed out the window.

"What." Deadpan serious but not that dumb.

"It snowed last night. It's cold. The wind is blowing . . ." My excuses met the resistance of his eyes and his glove, which he held outright, plaintively. It struck me how utterly ridiculous his request was. Playing catch in the cold snow in the dead whiteness of winter.

This would ruin my warm, cozy afternoon I had planned. There were a hundred reasons to hold firm. Only one to relent.

"Oil it up. I'll get the overalls."

We dressed warmly, layered and tight. Stocking hats—the kind with eye holes and a mouth hole that terrorists wear on the made-for-TV movies—covered our faces, masking our approach to this event. We trundled out into the snow, into the whip of the north wind that was trailing late behind the storm front now in eastern Iowa. The cold made our eyes water. We set up the game away from the deepest snow but near a finger drift that could pass for a shadow running south from a naked cottonwood.

"Don't drop the ball," I warned. "We might never find it in the snow." Game called on account of lost ball—a new wrinkle.

"I won't," he said, and he chucked the ball with a half toss, restricted by his winter clothing.

We were soon adjusting to the game, our sleeves pulled up slightly to loosen the clothing for more mobility around our shoulders.

Chad was inching toward the drift to the right. It was about two feet deep at its apex, a foot from the base of the tree. I could throw it to him there unobstructed. We had played this game before in the dry dirt of summer. I faked a throw to his left, then tossed it just far enough out of his reach to make him leap into the drift to catch it. He did, but it glanced off his glove and was buried.

We were digging in the drift and looking for the ball when his mom and sister drove up, back from grocery shopping in town. They stopped the truck, watched, shook their heads, and drove into the garage. *Just as well,* I thought. *I couldn't have explained this anyway.*

We found the ball and went back to tossing. Our body warmth

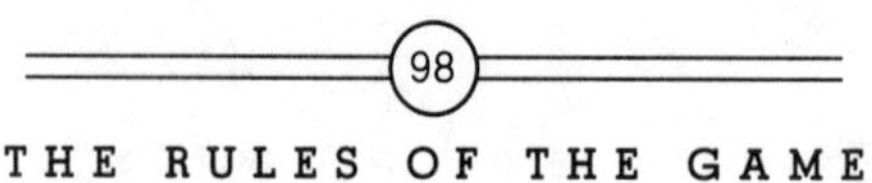

became enveloped inside the overalls; the chill lessened. Pop flies drifted in the wind, camouflaged against the white-gray sky. More the fun. As the day dipped over the horizon and night's blackness began to seep into the sky, we continued to toss the ball. Numbness dulled our hands and faces, and the ball stung, painful on each catch. Our hands finally became numb as we continued.

We both knew this was not baseball. Baseball has rules and fields and teams. This was not baseball. This was something else. It wasn't better, just different. I tossed the last throw high into the sky, and Chad lost it as it left my hand. We did not hear it hit the ground. He started to turn and look for it.

"Leave it," I said. "We'll get it next spring."

We went inside. I took off my clothes and went downstairs to warm up. The bottom half of my jeans were wet from snow. The fire had died out. Chad came down, having changed into a pair of dry sweats, and threw himself, red cheeked, onto the couch.

"Thanks, Dad," he said. And I was warm again.

"You cannot teach what you do not know, and you cannot lead where you will not go." Credit that to Merlin Carouthers, a powerful spokesman on religious matters. It applies to what we learn and what we pass on to our children. I wish I could say that the basics of baseball, the lessons of Little League, give us all the answers, but they don't. At times, for reasons inexplicable, we fail at the most basic task given a parent, the most basic responsibility accorded a father: giving your child a good example.

Now more than ever, children need to be shown, not told, the right way to live. Today they are too smart to be fooled by our blatant or even our hidden hypocrisy. Don't smoke, as we light up.

Don't drink, as we belt down another brew. Follow the rules, as we fudge on our taxes. Don't lie and don't steal. Then we smash their confidence by little indiscretions, while we convince ourselves that little means forgivable and unnoticed.

When we make a mistake, we throw up our hands and look at the glove and beg the question. Not "Why?" Answer that later when you've got an answer. The real question is "What next?" What next, because our children have had their expectations dashed. They now have only bad news. Their fluent, happy course of life has been derailed into a tangle of uncertainty, of mixed expectations, of fear. It's not as warm under the quilt anymore.

We can try to answer them. The changes caused by the act are irrevocable. They cannot be undone. You would give anything that it would not have happened, but it has. Hopelessly, you shrink into the selfish, childish blame of others, of yourself, as if life itself had stopped to allow you that indulgence.

Then quietly you are dragged back into the game by your children's eyes that cry out for an answer but recognize that there is none—eyes that offer forgiveness when none is deserved. They drag you back into the game because you realize there are more innings to play, the game is not over, and you still have an obligation to the team.

My dad turned seventy-six last Sunday. He and my mom came to visit me where I serve my sentence. We sat apart from the others, side by side, for three hours and talked. Pleasant, unstrained conversation. We talked about the farm, crops, weather, food, our health, and the future. Near the end of our three hours we grew silent, but it was not uncomfortable. We were past the point of forced conversation.

I thought back to the years past, to the times when we played ball and the times when we didn't. To the missed opportunities and botched plays we had left strewn across each other's lives.

When my dad left, he looked me in the eyes, and he felt what I felt, as my eyes looked into his. He saw what I saw when I looked into mine. And we remembered the lives we'd led separately, antithetical in both direction and purpose, having become circular as they had always been. That day, it mattered only that we both knew we wished we had played catch more often than we had, and that someday we would again.

10

EXTRA INNINGS

If you can look into the seeds of time, And say which grain will grow, And which will not, Speak then to me.

William Shakespeare, *Macbeth*

Age is a question of mind over matter. If you don't mind, it doesn't matter.

Leroy Robert "Satchel" Paige

Like it or not, the game of baseball was meant to be a finished product. By its very nature designed to have an ending, it therefore can go on forever. This may, at first blush, seem a contradiction, but it's not. Rather, it's one of those things that gives baseball its endearing familiarity.

Little League, most probably because of economic necessity, too little time, and too many teams, imposes an artificial time limit on some games. These limits are often ignored by teams and coaches who wish to avoid a long game, evenly played, ending in an artificial tie imposed by paper rules. A tie is an unfortunate expediency, or something your mother makes you wear to church on Sunday, and has no place in baseball.

I enjoy a blowout now and then. The kind of game that is over almost before it starts, where your team dominates in every area of the game and everyone plays well, coasting to easy victory. It's like a day at the office when the phone doesn't ring. But without question, the most satisfying games in which I have taken part have been nail-biting, nitty-gritty, extra-inning affairs where the outcome was obscured until the last out. Games that grabbed your gut and would not let go. Those are the games I best remember.

Down the right-field line, past the visitors bench, sharply southeast from first base, stands a scoreboard. It is fastened on one side to a large pole that holds up an array of six big lamps, and on the other side to a four-by-four post. The scoreboard, donated years ago, consists of a background of black plywood with two rows of white squares in the middle, which edge across the metal front of two rectangles painted "Home" and "Visitor." There are ten spaces for scores next to each team.

The scoreboard came from a local bottling company that still supplies the syrup to the concession stand, and it is an aged advertisement for Dr Pepper, the kind reminding you to have a Dr Pepper at 10:00, 2:00, and 4:00. Last year, a new electronic sign went up in left field, relegating this one to another diamond where it was still wanted.

There was a game when the ten spaces for inning scores were not nearly enough. It started innocently. A League game on a Thursday night. The weather was forgettable–another summer day blended into the dark of a late evening. We were playing a good team from Westfield that had beaten us early in the year on their home field. We were throwing our best pitcher, having rested J. C. Tuesday in a game we looked to win easily without him, and did.

We had gotten on the board early, in the first, on a walk, a single, and a sacrifice fly. We scored one, but we left one stranded when the rally petered out. A young girl, sister to one of the players, climbed a homemade ladder toting the metal *1* and *0* and slipped them into the grooves designated for the first inning. Their pitcher, settled down after a shaky start, looked smooth and strong, and a string of zeros were hung up concurrently in the second, third, and fourth.

In the top of the fifth, we found ourselves struggling with the excess of our own success. J. C., who had thrown hard and fast, had proven unhittable. He got cute with a curve, then another, and both were welcomed like a birthday and drilled into the outfield for extra base hits, scoring a run and leaving a man on second with no outs. I didn't need to go to the mound. I held my index finger up to our catcher. Fastballs, again effective, ended the threat, but the score was tied. We couldn't muster a hotdog, much less an assault, and we went weakly into the top of the sixth. We had not had a base runner for three innings and our bats were sleeping.

In the Little League, the sixth was supposed to be the last inning, and it was difficult to approach it in any other way. The intricate psychology of the last inning is lost on most Little Leaguers.

"Okay, guys, this is it," I explained, gathering the team before they went onto the field.

"This is what, Coach?" asked Brandon, a young player new to this game. Perhaps I hadn't explained, but it sure seemed clear enough.

"The last inning, Brandon. We need to hold 'em here." Now it was clear.

"If we don't hold 'em, we lose?"

"No . . . well, if we don't hold 'em and they score, then we lose. Gotta score to win." Okay, now it was clear.

"So, if they score a run, and we score a run, we win?"

"No." I was struck by how the other players appeared to follow this conversation but were still listening intently, except for a few who had probably asked the same questions before. "No, if we each score a run, we go to extra innings."

"Then what happens, Coach?"

"We start over, like a new inning. We do it again."

"How many innings do we play?" Brandon was getting it now.

"That depends." I knew that now was not the time to step in that quagmire, so I deftly avoided it, convincing myself that it did not matter. "Let's just play one inning at a time. I'll let you know when the game's over."

I'm not sure that satisfied Brandon. Probably not. I would explain it later, if I could. I would explain that I did not know how many innings it might take and how long the game might go on. I would explain that each team gets the same chances to score in their half of the inning as the other, so it was fair, but fairness did not ensure a successful result. I could not tell him how many extra innings we would play because it wasn't up to me; it was up to him and the other boys.

The sixth inning came and went like a cold shoulder. Neither team had embraced any runs, hits, or errors and the scoreboard looked like an exercise in binary mathematics. All artificial time barriers were gone. We had passed into the time warp, where everything is relevant to the last at bat. The game could go on ad infinitum, and there was nothing umpires, coaches, fans, not even mothers with cooling dinners, could do to stop the game. We were playing in a game that had breached its barriers and now had a life of its own.

I love extra innings as much as I fear them. They balance you precariously on the edge of victory, and you know that every play might be special, might be the play that ends the marathon. Yet, depending on which side of the scoreboard you are on, top or bottom, home or visitor, each half inning either starts or ends with hopeful anticipation. A missed scoring opportunity hurts in the top half, but it hurts more with a base runner on the bag in the bottom half. A score by the visitors in the top half is disheartening, but exhilaration abounds if you tie it up in the bottom. Each inning ends with nerve-racking anxiety.

Each play's importance is magnified, but can you say that a hit in the seventh or ninth was more important than an RBI double in the first? Passed opportunities are gone, yet sweating out infield hits, you wonder what you should have done differently earlier. Should you have bunted to start a rally? Should you have sent a runner from third? Will your pitcher last another inning? But realizing all of this means nothing except in retrospect. It leaves you to concentrate on the immediate, each pitch, each swing, each play.

Brandon didn't ask anything as we went back out onto the field in the top of the seventh. I didn't offer. Experience teaches from a solid syllabus. Rules implemented to keep a pitcher from overpowering a league, and to protect young arms, required me to pull J. C. after six, and I replaced him with Drew, who had been playing shortstop.

Drew took his warm-up pitches and began the inning. I had watched him warm up from the bench. He looked ready. His first pitch sailed high over the outreached pud of the catcher, striking the backstop five rows into the raised bleachers. I was wrong. Three more balls, and their lead runner was on.

"Drew, just ease up and throw strikes." I was on the mound.

Sure, he thought, *you relax and throw easy.*

"Okay," he said, and nodded his head.

He settled quickly into a rhythm and struck out the next two batters, but the runner advanced to second on a stolen base. Their next batter, a reserve, lifted a droopy fly over the infield and scored the runner from second. He then tried to advance to second himself, a mistake. The run crossed first, and the score was 2–1.

The boys settled uneasily into the bench and listened for the batting order. They understood the situation now, and Brandon explained it in the lucid language of Little League to those who didn't.

"We don't score, we're history!" and the boys around him nodded knowingly.

A sharp single, a walk, a line out, and a strikeout left men on first and second with two outs. Last chance, last out. Brian hit the ball on a line between third and short, and our lead runner scored ahead of the relay in from left field, but the catcher, alert to our base runners, threw quickly behind our man at third, ending the inning. 2–2. Top of the eighth. Not our last out. Not our last chance after all. We were alive.

Steadily, the ebb and flow of this extra inning struggle went on, high tide and low tide, scoring chances washed up on the beach like starfish, some scratched and saved, others washed back out to sea, lost in the vastness of their own kind. The girl at the scoreboard came running over in the top of the eleventh, frantic.

"I'm out of innings! What should I do?" I looked at the scoreboard, now lit by the artificial lighting, the sun having set an inning ago. The scoreboard was full.

"Well," pondering one of the duties of a coach, "just use the last box for each inning, and switch it if you need to. It shouldn't last much longer."

She thanked me and went back to her duty, climbing the ladder and removing the last zero in each box. At the end of the thirteenth, she put them back up again.

We had played two games plus an inning and had decided nothing except perhaps that now Brandon knew how it all worked. The game was not going to end. We would never stop. It would go on forever;

we would grow old here, marry, have children, and they would play in our places, endlessly, until time itself stopped. There would be no last inning, no final out.

I was convinced that the game was in charge tonight, that nothing could loosen its grip on me, on my boy, on my team. It would decide when to let go, when to let them all go home and be done with it.

In the top of the fourteenth, we went with our fourth pitcher. Four was all we had. Rod threw straight and accurate but not hard. I was sure we would give up a run or two, and we did. After an easy play at second for the first out, the center fielder, 0 for 7, broke his own slump with a long drive to right, and that was followed by a single, scoring him, and a double, scoring another. A walk and two steals put men at second and third. Their next batter hit a grounder back to Rod, who stabbed it with a backhand slap of his glove and threw it to Chad at home, who blocked the plate like he was guarding the last piece of pizza, stuffing him for the second out. The next batter, deflated, struck on three pitches. 4–2.

It was ours to win or lose, as if that cliché somehow was more applicable here than other games. Of course it was. I didn't have to tell the boys; they had heard a variation of it each inning until they told me with their gestures that they had heard enough. I sat back with the scorebook to watch. Quietly, I marked the events, the at bats in the bottom of the fourteenth.

Travis had advanced on a walk, and Bret singled him over to third. Dan lined a shot into left field, clearing the bases and tying the score. Our next batter Chad grounded to short and Dan was forced at second. Chad moved to second on a passed ball and to third on a sacrifice fly by Drew.

Brandon hit the ball, with Chad on third, right through the legs of the second baseman. Chad, running at the crack of the bat, slid in safely, not knowing of the error in the field—safe: 5–4. The game was over.

Brandon rounded first and seeing the crowd gathering like flies around Chad, trotted back in to join the celebration. I calmly put the scorebook down and walked into the melee, patting backs and giving hugs.

As was customary, both teams lined up to shake hands. This time, instead of simple obligatory congratulations, there were genuine congratulations all around. Like the time Pete Rose's Reds lost to Carlton Fisk's body-languaged home run in the twelfth inning of the sixth game of the World Series. Yet Rose said he was proud, even in defeat, to have taken part in such a contest.

I stopped the boy between whose legs the winning hit had rolled, and I took his hand. He barely looked up. "You played a fine game. Next game, you'll stop that ball."

He creased a smile and walked on.

The girl keeping score, too excited by the outcome, had forgotten to put up the last inning, and it looked like we were still playing, tied in the fourteenth. I left it up for the unbelieving.

The townsfolk who witnessed the game would talk about it at the coffee shop for a week. Brandon's granddad talked about it until football started in the fall. Brandon never mentioned it again.

We had battled back from behind a couple of times to tie the game, so we could stay alive, with a chance to win. The extra innings were like that—fair and equal, another chance to succeed. Win or lose, you can't fault the game, since you always had the chances. Time stood still, waiting for you to catch up. "Come on" it said, "you're falling behind." Faster and faster you ran, until you were almost even again with it. Sometimes it didn't wait, and you lost it, falling behind. But it was always there, standing, jauntily leaning James Dean-like, against the storefront around the corner. And off you'd go again.

That day, after fourteen innings, we'd come out ahead, but tomorrow might be different. We knew that because we learned it. While it was nice to win, we also learned that anything can happen when you play the game and you've got to play the game for anything to happen.

11

MEN IN BLUE

The Lord openeth the eyes of the blind.

Psalm 146:8

That's what it means to be an umpire. You have to be honest, even when it hurts.

Doug Harvey,
major league umpire,
after a member of his umpiring
crew admitted an error

Umpiring a Little League baseball game may be the most selfless act a person can do for young athletes. Thankless because by umpiring's very nature, the best umpires remain unseen, hidden and obscured by their own competence. If an umpire becomes the focus of attention in a game, he (or she) has lost effectiveness. So it is that the best umpires never get thanked, since after doing a good job, no one can see any reason to thank them. Yet no actor plays a more important role in the honest flow of the game.

I call them actors—most good umpires have a flair for the dramatic. They realize there are a number of ways to do their job. Having some fun by participating in the activity, rather than merely observing it, is one method. The major league has many umpires schooled in the performing arts, shooting down runners at first like hired guns, emphatically exiting with a loaded finger those out on base. The pregnant pause can be used in extemporaneous speech and just as effectively after a clear strike, freezing a batter with indecision, then ending his uncertainty with an explanatory point at the outside corner. Most umpires who enjoy their job show it in their improvisational theatrics.

It is not, however, all fun. An umpire's job is a difficult one. A close play at first is inevitable, and if the umpire watches the ball into the glove instead of the runner's foot onto the bag, he'll miss the call.

The acute use of all the senses is necessary for effective play calling. Sight and sound are joint assistants in the tools of the umpire's trade. Hearing the ball into the first baseman's glove while watching the runner's foot approach the bag is required on a close play. In Little League, where two umpires is normal instead of three or four, an ump may be required to see two bases almost simultaneously, anticipating the prospective play and the location of the ball. Constant movement on the field, adjusting positions and angles even as the ball redirects their motion once again, is the norm for a successful umpire.

There are schools for umpires—training grounds that teach fundamentals to those who call the plays. But few Little League umpires go—most are parents, volunteers, and brothers of players who get drafted out of the stands. They do their best, yet their best is often less than everyone expects, owing to their volunteer status. That is how it should be.

Since so many umpires are untrained volunteers, I feel obliged to offer some suggestions, a list of "commandments" if you will, though not from the mount, to aid those part-timers in their effort. Not etched in anything resembling granite, here is but a first attempt to provide some help to those who in their own benevolence offer their help to the young boys and girls who play the game of baseball.

1. Thou Shalt Make Up Thy Mind

When you see a play, make up your mind and call it as you see it as soon as you see it. You may not always be right, but you'll be understood, which is nearly as important. The reason is simple. There are at least eighteen sets of ears whose reaction depends entirely on your call, and if it is indecisive, the play stops and waits. That is not good.

Our boys were playing away one afternoon on a field where the first-base line seemed to fade out as it wandered out to right field. It was nearly impossible to see.

We were up, and the bases were full. Bret sprayed a hit high up the right-field line, over first base, and it landed on or near that line just described. The boys on the bases began running, listening for the red light of the umpire if the ball was foul. A fair ball is always silent; only if the ball is not in play are any words spoken. As the ball landed, the umpire moved even with what looked like the foul line.

His right arm shot right of first base, and he yelled, "Foul!" then again, immediately, though not as loudly, "Fair!"

The boys, strung out between bags like worry beads on a taut line, stopped and looked to the umpire for further advice. It was not forthcoming. Perhaps embarrassed, he turned his back Pilate-like on the players, and stood mute. The right fielder threw the ball into second, who tagged the runner, then to short, who tagged the second runner, now immobile, and onto third, who ran down the third runner. A triple play, not caused by the excellence of execution but by the indecision of the umpire. Make the call, right or wrong. If you want to correct it later, do so if you find it in error, but don't leave the players hanging on your words.

2. Thou Shalt Speak Loudly

Baseball is a game designed to be played with your mouth as much as with anything else. This is not chess. Talking to each other, telling positions, and calling off catches is part of the game for the

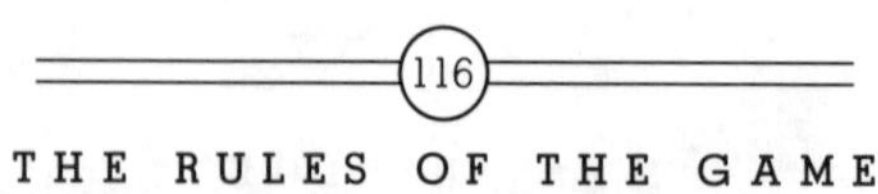

players. It's that way because catching the ball in the field is difficult business that requires the full attention of the defensive player. Someone else on the team but not in the play has to act as your eyes, lest you take them off the ball, dooming your chance to catch it.

Just as important, the umpire must be heard. A called strike, ball, safe or out, fair or foul, if not audible, is best not made. The senses are acceptable substitutes for each other in the game, and the minds of young boys and girls can be developed to allow them to hear and see alternately, when necessary, that which they need to see and hear. When the call made can't be heard or understood, the flow of the game stops in its tracks.

An umpire should be loud and distinct. You are a beacon to the children of summer, and a dim light is more dangerous than helpful. The players want to listen to the call, not watch it, and move into the play confident of their reaction. Speak up.

3. Thou Shalt Understand the Rules

Everyone wants to help out when asked, to be a part of the process, and in Little League, volunteers are essential. Parents and relatives, pulled out of the stands, asked to serve as officials on the field, generally do. A word of advice. If you don't understand the rules, politely defer.

It is no shame to admit you do not fully know the rules; they are not so easily understood. They are to a great extent situational, requiring the same kind of reaction that players themselves must develop during years of playing. For umpires it is no different, and if the rules are obscure or obtuse, reaction to a situation on the field will be impossible to implement and generally wrong.

Take, for instance, the infield-fly rule. I have been involved as player and coach in Little League for years, and that rule still twists my mind. When does it apply? When do we call it? Man on first and second—how many outs?

And what about a batter who hits the ball, and it hits him as he leaves the batter's box? Safe or out? Or the base runner who passes another on the base path then finds the man ahead of him tagged out? Who's on first?

Study the game and learn the rules. Watch the situations, go over them in your mind, learn to react. Work a game or two with an experienced umpire, one you can rely on; make joint decisions, asking for help when you need it. Get a rule book and read it. Once you develop your confidence in the book, it will be easier for you in the field. Then have at it. You are needed in blue.

4. Thou Shalt Admit Thy Mistakes

You might get a lot of disagreement on this one, but stick to your guns. If you make a mistake and can correct it, do it. Let me tell you why I think so.

The game is for the kids, not the parents or fans. Kids who play Little League are not dumb. They are aware when mistakes are made. I have umpired games in which I have made a call in the field that, upon reflection or better viewing, was just plain wrong. I have

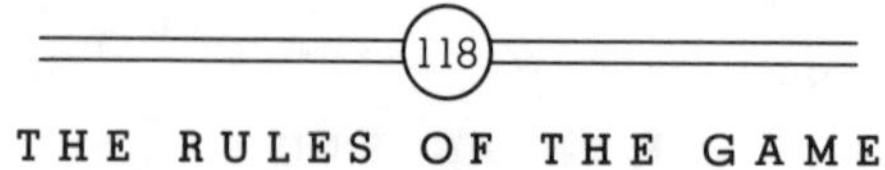

learned to change my mind. A dropped ball that first appeared caught, a missed tag that first appeared promptly placed, a foot pulled off first base on a close play. The kids know what's what, and they would rather have the right call than the first call, even if it goes against them.

Plus, it teaches kids fairness. And if Little League and baseball can't teach fairness, they ought not teach anything. Fairness is not an easy concept to learn, and at every opportunity a child should have an example of its operation, an occasion to learn its effect and impact. Admitting a mistake, openly, in front of the world—or at least a small section of it—is perhaps the simplest way to do that. When adults admit mistakes, it ratifies the acceptability of such admissions in the children who may be more inclined to hide from the duty of repentance.

If you are umping a game and you realize that you have made a mistake that can be corrected fairly within the active context of the game, do so. If it can't be, at least admit your error to the coach or players involved. They will appreciate your honesty and learn that missed calls and mistakes are a part of the fabric of the game.

5. Thou Shalt Remember Thy Place on the Field

An umpire can be as much of an obstacle as a rough infield can. Know your place. Watch your position in relation to the other players, and avoid as much as possible getting in their way. There are certain places to stand so as to avoid awkward, direct conflict with a fielder. You do not want to be in the way of a play, yet you need to be in a position to make the call.

With no runner on, position yourself behind first base, down the right-field line. You can make a foul call and move over to watch the play at first. With a runner on first or second, move in behind the pitcher so as to permit the infielder free view throughout the diamond, yet still allow you access and open observation to first, second, and third, depending on where the play occurs.

Be invisible, at least as far as possible. Out of the way yet ready to act. Your job is to help keep the order, not write the story. A gentle touch, not a heavy hand.

6. Thou Shalt Not Embarrass a Player

We all like to watch the colorful major league umpires. They, by demand, have become part of the entertainment of the game. One umpire, drawing his hand and index finger like a six-shooter, executes the base runners as outs each inning. Others, dramatic and fluent, actually rehearsed and refined, call a third strike like the announcement of a major find. That's okay for adults playing a game that has become a business. Kids are different.

Emphatic, dramatic exclamations of failure—for that is precisely much of what the umpire does—are hurtful to some children and should be avoided at all cost. A shouted, exuberant "Strike Three!" with a fanciful flourish might make you the ump feel important, but it can be an unfair weight on the shoulders of a small boy. To him, strike three is a failure, so temper your announcement. To him, an out is a lost opportunity, so silence your delight.

Realize that your job is to provide the details, the facts, impartial and straight, a blank wall, not a barbed-wire fence. It is not out of line for an umpire at that level to congratulate and recognize the effort, even if subpar or failed. A lot can be gained if after "Out," you throw in "Nice try, kid."

7. Thou Shalt Educate the Players

Little League is a school. The game is new to many and the language foreign. The rules and situations are complex and ever changing. An umpire should offer help to a young player who needs it.

I knew a young boy to whom "Tag on a fly" was no clearer than talking in tongues. I would yell at him from the coach's box; he would nod his head understandingly, then take off as soon as the ball was hit high up into the air, thus ensuring a double play against our team. It was some time before I understood he did not know what *tag* meant, and in retrospect that was understandable. This baseball slang, this vernacular, was new to him. I looked up the word "tag" in the dictionary, and it was variously defined as "to follow closely or persistently," "to keep close," and "to hit solidly." Nowhere was there a definition that compelled him to stay snug on the base and only advance the instant the ball was caught. No one had explained it to him, taking for granted that the language of baseball came somehow at an early age without instruction.

An umpire in the field sees many small violations of the rules,

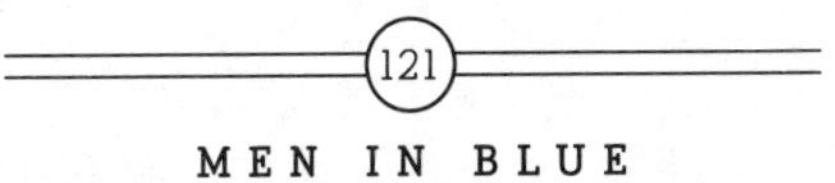

most out of ignorance. Take a moment, explain the violation, couch it as a "warning," if you must, but if possible, explain before the act of punishment. The goal is to teach, not impeach.

8. Thou Shalt Let the Play on the Field Decide the Game

This one is difficult, even in the abstract. Understandably, you have a job to do. This commandment does not suggest you sublimate your job to a goal of nonintervention. This is after all, a game of baseball, not diplomacy. Yet I have seen even the best-intentioned umpires act in such a way that their actions and their call of the game began to and ultimately succeeded in overshadowing the game itself. No one came to watch you umpire.

This requires intuitive skill and discipline. You must learn how and when to exert your control over the game by implementation of the rules you are expected to enforce. At the same time, you must recognize when a rigid and strict enforcement of those same rules begins to stifle the competitive juices of the players involved in the game.

Do you call a runner out who, while using his best efforts to dodge a hit ball, steps briefly out of the base path? Do you shrink the strike zone to the size of a postage stamp? Is a ball caught in center field after a long run, held for a few moments and then dropped, any less an out? The object is to let the kids go home realizing they either won or lost on their own, by their own honest effort. Stay low, and consider the kids. There is no harm in that.

9. Thou Shalt Keep Thy Cool

Henry Ford once said, "A man will never forgive you for the wrongs he has done to you." So it is with the indolent and irate parents and fans.

Apart from barring all parents from their children's games, which, if only in its simplicity, has some merit, about the only course an umpire can take when the complaining starts is to ignore it. This is not easy, for no man likes to suffer indignity in silence. A volunteer should not expect to be insulted, nor should he accept it with uncompromising grace.

But strangely, umpires are more akin to authority figures, and therefore more subject to abuse than other similar volunteers. It is a sad commentary on the state of our attitudes that we permit this to continue.

Later, I will say more about the parent as fan, that subject requiring more comprehensive treatment than is acceptable here. Suffice it to say that from the umpire's point of view, the less said the better. Do your best job, stay calm, explain to the participants a disputed call and your reason for making it (always keeping in mind the fourth commandment), and ignore the fans outside the fence.

Most decent fans are embarrassed by a heckler. Hecklers are rarely embarrassed. Given those postulates, ignoring a heckler will eventually ostracize him into silence or isolation. Either will serve your purpose.

As for rude participants in the game, only throw coaches or players out of the game if after repeated and rude violations of decorum,

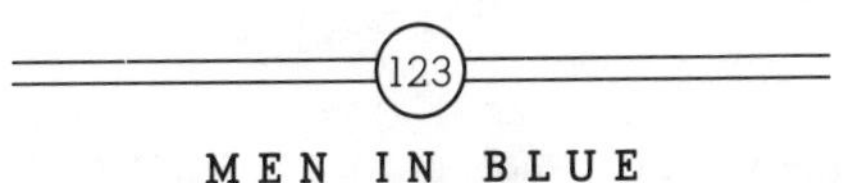

you ask them if they want to be thrown out and they reply, either directly or indirectly, "Yes." Even the most recalcitrant will fail to respond to this warning, and only the dimmest will miss your meaning.

10. Thou Shalt Remember When Thou Was Young

Adults ruin much of what they touch, even inadvertently. Little League is a child's game, but adults take it over like it somehow still belongs to us. We try to make it into what we remember we used to want. Our memories are usually jaded, but even if not, what right do we have to usurp our children's opportunities and their game as our own? Our time has passed; it is their game now. Consider:

> Then he was home again. Perhaps he expected to be punished upon his return, for what, what crime exactly, he did not expect to know, since he had already learned that, though children can accept adults as adults, adults can never accept children as anything but adults too.
>
> William Faulkner, *Light in August*

I have called these commandments, but that's presumptuous. Let's call them suggestions instead, small ideas that work to help adults understand their place in the game their children have adopted. The men in blue, the cops of the diamond, are there to enforce the rules. They are also there to help keep the memories of the adults who occupy themselves offstage sober and consistent—

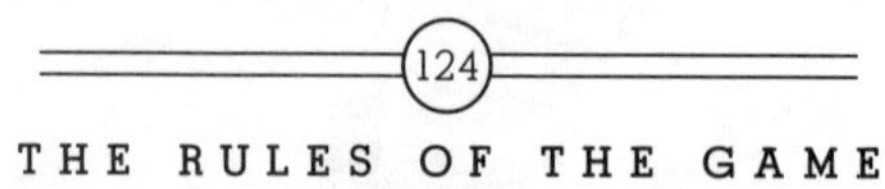

consistent with the goals of the game. Serve if you will. Umpire if you are able and called. Remember your place in the field of play and, as much as possible, stay out of the way. There are children playing baseball.

12

ON LOSING

I realize the utter futility of self-pity. Success and failure are never final, and neither count for very much in the final assessment of any man who has done his best.

AA, *The Big Book,* The Career Officer

The first time anyone suggested to these boys that they must come to love each other while they were on the field, they laughed uneasily at the idea. Now they don't laugh. After enduring the Hampton Horns together, they seem to understand—at least, a little.

Stephen King,
reporting on his son's Little League baseball team

Probably no experience in American culture, especially American sports culture, has been so unfairly denigrated as losing. Thanks to the uneven prism of professional sports, losing has come to represent the essence of failure. The attitude is that if you do not win, you fail, and no one out of first place has achieved anything lastingly important.

This attitude unfortunately carries over, like many sports idioms, into the games of youth. The attitude is brought there mostly through the seeping, insatiable expectations of adults, whose own lives remain empty until their progeny grow up to act where they themselves have fallen short. We want our children to win because we did not, and somehow their success will assuage our own lack of it.

Sadly, the statistics simply don't work that way. Everyone fails and fails regularly in some fashion or another. Sport, more particularly baseball, is the clearest example of that truism. Failure in baseball is so commonplace that we oftentimes fail to recognize it, our expectations having been dramatically reduced.

Winning is but a part of baseball. The whole is the experience gained from learning, and learning involves losing as much as winning. Only by taking the whole with the part can we gain real perspective of the nature of both success and failure. Each at bat, each inning, each game, each series, each season throughout a lifetime of seasons, can be put under the scalpel and dissected. More often than not, failure is rampant, out of control. Yet life, as in baseball, often gives you another chance.

Take, for example, a simple at bat. The object, of course, is to hit the thrown ball into the field of play where it won't be touched and retrieved before you can run to first base and beyond. A relatively simple assignment on its face. Yet even the most successful fail at that task twice as often as they succeed. Grant that ratio to a trial lawyer, a doctor, or a schoolteacher and they will soon be looking for work in some other field.

Then comes the question of when to measure the indicators of success: after the first at bat, at the end of the game, at the end of the season, or at the end of the career? It is not that the indicators can't be measured variably on a continuum or cut out like pieces of a time line, short and abrupt. They can. Neither are fair and accurate, yet both are. The problem is not in the time line chosen, but in the indicators of success we accept as a measure of achievement. Baseball thankfully allows us the opportunity for another at bat and hopeful chances after each defeat. As long as you keep playing, you get another chance, another opportunity to swing the stick and walk away from your last at bat a winner.

The closeness of the moist August night swallowed us whole. June bugs, beyond the end of their tenure, floated into the mercury lamp hung high. Solitary crickets sang to each other, a mixed chorus, across the green expanse of the outfield.

We had traveled north into the lakelands of Minnesota, to Thief River Falls, for a year-end tournament. Our caravan, our team of Little Leaguers from our Little League town in Nebraska, had ventured to the tournament. These tournaments were special, a season-ending surprise, more vacation than vocation. We meant to enjoy ourselves around a baseball tournament, and whole families had taken a few days off to travel into the Land of 10,000 Lakes. We would play at least two games—more if we kept winning.

A steel structure behind the grassy infield covered in dark green tin jutted up from the raw Minnesota plains. The silvery glare of the structure was softened next to the warm, brown infield and freshly cut grass. The bleacher seats, keen and glistening, would hold a bigger crowd than had ever seen our boys play before. At the top of the structure and centered between four flights of seats rose the box, a glass-enclosed setting, green enameled and sparkling, in which sat announcers, scorekeepers, and the lone newswriter who would cover the tournament for the local weekly, *The Prairie Sentinel.*

Our caravan circled the field, driving onto the blacktopped parking lot under the "Welcome to Thief River Falls—Joe Nadir Ballpark" sign. We parked near the front of the lot and began emptying the cars and vans of players, families, and equipment.

The boys, awed by the sight of the ballpark, scurried off in twos and threes to explore the new land. Mothers and fathers stretched their legs under the bright midwestern sky, holding fast to our uneven dreams of execution and hope. We entered the arena unaware of events to be exposed to us in which we were to play a prominent role.

Our first game was an evening affair, scheduled to start about seven, depending on the outcome of the game scheduled at four-thirty. We would wait and watch as the other teams played. From up in the stands we could look down on a setting so perfect that it seemed surreal. Boys in colorful uniforms worn in honor of the towns that sent them were out on the grass, tossing the white spheres back and forth, looking smaller than they were, young, ebullient, and alive. I sat in a slight breeze watching. I wished I were twelve again.

When we realize we are not twelve, yet want to be, we often become through our children what we wish to be but never were. It is a dangerous desire. In its hold, we seek what we ought not have and take from our children their chance to have what we missed. We push our children to do what we have been unable to do. If they too fail, as many do, partly because the goal is not theirs and partly because the goal is itself unattainable, they will grow older and push just as blindly, toward a different goal, seen through their eyes, just as unattainable, bereft of ownership.

I admit this error. In my case, at least, it is an error of good intention. Some of the most damaging are. The secret is to stop your childhood where it ended, and that is a most difficult task. In baseball it is doubly difficult since the game does not lend itself to easy demarcation between childhood play and adult competition.

The line of demarcation is rarely black and straight. More often than not, it is black, then gray, then white. No easy rule nor parable nor proverb will tell you where the white ends and black begins—that you must learn for yourself. On our trip to Thief River Falls, I had not yet learned the lesson of the line.

On the second day we found ourselves, to our surprise, with three wins and waiting to see who we would play for the championship. We had not expected this easy success, and we wore it uncomfortably. We had played nearly flawless ball, and the bounces and calls had gone our way. Now we sat and watched the other bracket play-off to determine who we would face in the final game—either the local favorite or the team from New Ulm. We had played and beaten the team from New Ulm early that morning. The local team had won, we were told, the Joe Nadir league championship that summer, and they were the favorite in this tournament.

Joe Nadir, locally famous but regionally obscure, was like one of a thousand hometown heroes, who had settled comfortably in Thief River Falls and dedicated himself to making the local ball program better. During that weekend, I had learned that he had played minor league ball, spent a brief stint with a Chicago club, though I never learned which one, ruined his arm either pitching or in a barroom fight, drank excessively or not at all, married money, and had become part of local legend. Despite the incongruity of version, clearly he had spent a good part of this last ten years creating an environment in this small northland town where baseball was welcome, even worshiped. He was dead now, but baseball lived on.

Our game, as expected, ended up being against the local team. They had beaten New Ulm 6–4 with a rally in the last inning. We warmed up in the heat of that August night. The boys seemed anxious to play.

It is the memory of that game, of the events of that August night, that has led me to this story. For in its retelling I can purge, somewhat, from my own mind the consequence that haunts me. I still learn from the retelling, but the retelling is a painful act. It may also be helpful—like physical therapy on a wounded limb—but it is nevertheless painful. It haunts me by constantly reminding me of my own mistake. I know too that my mistake was neither innocent nor harmless.

The details fade into the action, but this much is certain. Our good fortune continued into the championship game. Pitching was sharp, honed by a season of work and tuned by the last day and a half of confident success. Our defense played flawlessly, and our hitting sparkled. By the end of the fourth inning, we were ahead 6–1 and growing in confidence.

We had come for a good time, and now the tournament looked to be ours, which would have been an unexpected and surprising achievement beyond our dreams. Our local boys having traveled far from home to face premier competition were on the verge of proving themselves equal to the task.

At this stage of the game, up big in the late innings, the substitutes were usually inserted. I hesitated. We had four boys who had not yet played. They were the same boys who often sat during the season, waiting their turn, but always there in practice. They had gotten better during the season, but they were still not our best fielders and batters. They would not be easy to hide in either place. I was concerned at upsetting the flow of the game that seemed to have gone our way so far.

"Coach, when will I go in?" It was Jason. He was asking me what I had avoided answering myself. I mentally computed outs in my lineup, contemplating a substitution where the odds of an at bat for Jason were diminished.

"I'll let you know." Jason, pulling on his hat, sat back down.

I could justify my decision in my own mind. I'd know more in another inning; things would be clearer. We couldn't afford a letdown now. The game was going too well. It wouldn't be fair to give up a chance to win it all, the championship, the big enchilada, after having gotten so close. It wouldn't be fair to the boys. I effused excuses.

We struggled in the sixth inning, scoring no runs and giving up three. With just an inning left, I felt vindicated. The score stood 6–4 in our favor, and it could have been much worse had I made the substitutions in the last inning. *Yes,* I thought, *I need to do the right thing for the boys.*

"Coach?" Jason was on his feet in the dugout, seeking an answer. The other three boys, willing participants, now abject spectators, looked my way, waiting.

"Are we gonna bat?"

"We'll see. We need a few insurance runs. If we get them, I'll put you in." I was resolute. This tournament did not require me to play all the players equally. It was up to me.

The game ended quickly; it was almost a blur. Jason got as far as the on-deck circle, and our last out sent him back to the bench. Three quick fly outs ended the game. Jubilant, we were champions. The celebration, the screaming, the backslapping congratulations of parents and boys, started after the last out and carried us off the field into a park area, where our fans and players broke out into an impromptu picnic, roasting hot dogs, drinking Cokes, and relishing and rerelishing every play.

We had won it all—we had set out against the odds and succeeded. I felt satisfied and complete in the team's success. Although just the coach, the win was mine too, I thought. I had taken these boys through practices starting in the wet cold of a Nebraska April through this glorious hot August night of victory. I felt good.

I grabbed a hot dog and walked over to a bench near a shade tree where my son was sitting. The park lights were turned off, and only the dim glow of the walkway lamps and the coals of the grills illuminated our crowd.

"Nice game, Chad."

"Thanks." He swallowed a Coke. Our quiet silence spoke volumes.

"Quite a tournament."

He agreed. Out of the corner of my eye, I noticed Jason and another boy approach, holding a can of pop in their hands. Jason was eating a hot dog.

"Jason." I called to him and he walked over to where I was sitting.

"How's the hot dog?"

He smiled. "Pretty good." Jason liked to eat.

"Think you'll ever forget this game?" I asked more seriously.

"What do you mean?" He looked puzzled.

"Nothing. Forget it. Enjoy your Coke." They walked away.

"Can you figure those guys?" I asked Chad, still munching on the relish-covered dog. "Biggest game of the year and they act like it was nothing."

"They didn't play," he said. He didn't accuse; it was simple and straightforward, matter of fact.

The game didn't mean to them what it meant to me, what I expected it to mean to them, because they hadn't been given an opportunity to invest part of themselves in the experience. They weren't angry. They weren't upset. They were, instead, benched, by me and my altruistic logic: Win first for the boys. I thought that they did not know, but they did.

We had won the prize, but in the process I had lost sight of why we came to play. I took from four boys an experience they would not get back. I realized then, clearly and unmistakenly, that there are times in your life where you long to turn back the clock and undo what you have done. Those moments may pass by, flitting by unnoticed in the great black expanse of your mind like fireflies in the open night, or they may simmer then burn brightly, scarring your mind with a hot, white brand. But either way, they pass by and are irretrievably gone, lost at the outer edge of your life, where black turns to gray turns to white.

So afraid of losing, wanting so badly to win, I had forgotten the purpose of success. My job as a coach, and a father, was to provide for the boys a learning opportunity, a chance to enjoy each other, and a time to explore their own abilities and challenge their spirits through the game of baseball.

Losing meant nothing if the challenge was faced head-on by each of them and if they, in the giving of the best effort they had to offer, knew they had done the best they could do. Instead I had taught four boys, by my own prejudice and misplaced pride, that winning was more important than the effort spent to achieve it.

The Coke dripped condensation off my hand and onto my chest as I finished it off, draining it into my parched, dry throat. I threw the rest of the hot dog away. They tried to put the championship trophy in my van, but I begged off, placing it in the neighbor's instead. We loaded up the equipment, the boys, the fans, and the memories and drove off into the empty blackness of that Minnesota night, savoring a victory that had left a bitter taste in my mouth. I drove all night, alone, me and my mistake, as everyone else in the van slept. I had seen in that languid August night, finally, that line of demarcation between childhood play and adult competition, too late to comprehend what it was and too proud to understand what it meant.

13

COACHING KIDS

For all we have and are,
For all our children's fate,
Stand up and take the war,
The Hun is at the gate!

Rudyard Kipling, "For All We Have and Are"

A team is where a boy can prove his courage on his own. A gang is where a coward goes to hide.

Mickey Mantle

Given all the critical books and articles written about the nature of Little League coaching, you would think that the majority of coaches were a cross between Jack LaLane and Herman Goering. Actually, my experience has been quite the opposite. Most of the coaches I've met and battled are generally well intentioned, knowledgeable about the game, and concerned for their players. No doubt, there are those who possess no sympathy or concern, as there are in every aspect of life, and their actions on the field of play pull down the average. Yet even without grading on a curve, I'd give most Little League coaches high marks.

It takes something different to coach kids—young, impressionable, awkward, learning, growing kids. They come to you as a package, not one of those sorted-by-machine-evenly-cut-out-all-the-same-size-and-shape packages. Rather, they come to you as varied and different as a handful of hope. Boys and girls, even near the same age, are not the same size or shape, nor do they possess the same maturity or skill. Each child comes unfinished, in differing stages of development, and your task is to bring together those pieces so that the finished product resembles a unit, still varied and individual, yet cohesive.

You can't mass-produce a baseball team. That's why coaching is more art than profession, more a love than a vocation.

Find me someone who doesn't love being patient with the exasperation of young children, and you'll soon see what not to be in a coach. Push too hard to make the piece fit and you're liable to break or damage it. Better to put two pieces next to each other, so that the gentle, and often not so gentle, scrape and clash of a season will wear them into a close approximation of a fit. That is what you must settle for.

You will see coaches, even experienced ones, who do not comprehend this principle. They coerce, antagonize, and verbally pound their team, hoping to change the child to fit the slot. Stop, coaches; you are wasting your time.

You may counter with stories of success that your method imparts, stories that counter my advice with examples of how hard practice created something from nothing, where your "pounding" created a fit for a vacant hole. And I may be hard-pressed to argue that your method did not achieve a measure of success. But at what price was it achieved? Is the child better off? Is the team? There are, to my mind, times when a hard approach is needed to mold or correct a rough edge of personality. But baseball is a game, and I do not believe that in that arena the hard approach consistently applied to young children will result in the goals we are challenged to achieve.

At this moment, Leo Durocher is spinning and the hue and cry is rising. Remember though, before you accept Leo "the Lip" at his word, whom I happen to appreciate for his unusual candor, that he didn't coach many Little Leaguers when he said these things about coaching and baseball: "Nice guys finish last"; and "Some guys are admired for coming to play, as the saying goes. I prefer those who come to kill." These remarks were attributed to Durocher during his twenty-four-year career as manager with the Dodgers, Giants, Cubs, and Astros. They are, to be sure, fair and accurate assessments of what it takes at that level.

Unfortunately, as is our habit in America, we recklessly apply a perfectly legitimate approach in one field to another, without regard for its effect or suitability. What worked for Sam Walton may not work at all for a mom-and-pop grocery.

The problem is a deep-seated distrust of our own intuition. We do not believe what we feel to be true unless it coincides with the opinion of an expert on the subject. Careful reflection will reveal how many times that has happened to you. You attend a movie panned by critics, and you feel ashamed to admit that, well, you liked it. You buy a car *Consumer Reports* raved about, but it turns out to be a lemon. You buy a best-seller because it's a best-seller, but are quickly bored by it. All of this can be done, harmlessly, with books and cars and movies.

Children playing baseball are different. Boys playing Little League baseball are different still. That is why I consider coaching those boys something akin to a high obligation, a duty carrying with it honor and respect, imparting much in return. To treat it as something less is to denigrate the subject as much as the teacher. A coach cannot be less of a man to his players than he is to his own son.

That is nothing if not difficult. All the sage advice I might impart would consist mostly of stories where I have failed to do as I have suggested be done. It is tough work because, stripped to its bare bones, coaching requires first that the coach understand what it means to be a man, and second that the coach understand what it means to teach boys how to become men.

Across America today, the contemporary classrooms of life are full of needy students waiting for a curriculum. In a lot of homes, they are waiting for the teacher. The daunting task cannot be avoided, however compounded the difficulties. As long as there are boys to be coached, we must not stop the coaching.

Example teaches lasting lessons. The memories of my coaches, from which I have learned much, are not so much of instruction as involvement. By somehow becoming a part of my life, even a small part, their influence over me has been disproportionately great. These were men who did not sit on the sidelines and call plays, although they did do that too; they were men who bumped and ground and pushed and shoved, then picked us up off the hard ground when we fell, dusted off our backsides, and showed us what to do.

They were men who knew how to laugh at what was funny and how to cry at what was sad. These were men who bled from cut lips or bumped noses, and they knew how it hurt when it happened to you. These were men who experienced pain and defeat, joy and success, and balanced the beams enough to keep the lows high and the highs low. They remembered what had happened to them when it happened to you.

I was in a slump. The mother of all slumps. Slump-o-rama. It was early March. I was a senior in high school, and I was playing basketball. Our team was eventually headed for the Nebraska state tournament in Lincoln. Our school was Class D, the small school division in Nebraska. Homer had never sent any team to any state tournament. We were going–but we didn't know it then.

We had to play three games in district play and then win a regional contest to qualify for the state tournament. Only eight small schools statewide would go.

I played forward on an evenly talented team of miscreants—now they call them free spirits. Our head coach was all business; he commanded respect and deserved it. He was intelligent, and while he recognized our loose team personality, he never gave in to it when the game was close. He required discipline, made us run our plays, directed our traffic and our mouths. He was most responsible for our success.

But the coach I remember best was our assistant coach, barely more than a kid himself. He was two years out of college, big and physical, and his personality laughed out loud. We never called him anything but "Coach," even in the classroom, where he taught American history like an afterthought. He was generous with his compliments if we needed a shot of self-esteem. But when we bellied up to the bar of self-pride, he would cut us down with a quiet but cutting comment, neither offered in malice nor permanently wounding. He encouraged the balance between demanding execution and expecting excellence, knowing intrinsically that one comes with the other but that at times both are out of reach.

It was districts, and I was in a slump. Lately, my shooting had left something to be desired. Every shooter experiences a slump, just as every batter does. At some stage in the season your mechanics, on which you have religiously relied throughout the year, become distinctly unmechanical. You are lost, floundering under the weight of your own inability, and the only way to overcome it, to break out, is to keep doing exactly what you've been doing. Beat the devil and the law of averages into submission. Those of you who have tried to beat those foes realize that they are beaten on faith alone, and not easily at that.

I was in the slumpiest of slumps. To say that I had been cold the last few games is to say Lenin was a Communist. When I walked down the hall during school, my friends bundled up. My idea, born of self-pity, was to quit shooting the ball. You can't hurt what you don't feel. Coach, however, had a different plan.

He could have tried to coax me into shooting the ball by gentle verbal persuasion. He could have built up my confidence by rigorous, repetitive practice until my slump slacked off. He could have tried to work on my mechanics, analyzing my technique and altering it ever so slightly until I was back in form. But instead, he did the only thing that could have worked on my seventeen-year-old head. He got me mad.

The Saturday before districts started, we practiced in the large gymnasium at the high school. It was familiar and warm, and the rich, shiny, light-brown hardwood welcomed us into practice. I had come off a stellar four-for-fifteen shooting night in a final season win. Two of the baskets that went in were accidents. I was in a deep shooter's depression, the kind where you slowly commit suicide by beginning to miss free throws. All of my old familiar shooting spots on the home court had abandoned me, like friends after a conviction, until I was alone and disoriented.

Coach challenged me to a game of one-on-one. He was a better than good athlete, and I probably had no better than a fifty-fifty chance to beat him on my best day. That was not my best day. Coach proceeded to shoot, drive, and generally humiliate me into one lopsided defeat after another. He never said a word, never offered any criticism, nor for that matter, any compliment. When I wanted to stop, he would insist we play one more game. I went zero for Saturday.

In the showers after practice, I tried to wash it all off. Our opening round game was Monday night, and the only thing that stood between me and public humiliation was church on Sunday. As I sat on the bench in front of my screened red locker, drying off and putting on my pants, Coach sauntered over. I looked up. He was not smiling.

"Keep shooting the ball." He said it like he meant it.

I thought he was crazy.

"Right," I answered sarcastically.

"Keep shooting the ball." He repeated it and turned away.

I'd never thought of him as obscure, but I had no idea what he meant. I was convinced he meant something else and that the water still in my ears had deceived me.

Monday night rolled into town, and we won easily, scoring over eighty points. I had five. Once, during a particularly bad moment, I had shot the ball from about eighteen feet, my usual range, and hit the top of the backboard, bouncing the ball into the dark green curtain on the stage behind the backboard. Not a command performance. My teammates left me alone after the game, like when you see a strange stray dog rummaging in the garbage can—you hope he goes away before he makes a mess, but you are a little wary of chasing him off yourself. We wouldn't play again until Thursday night, and if we won, the finals would be Friday night. We would practice again Tuesday after school.

Again on Tuesday and Wednesday, before our routine, Coach put me through the one-on-one drill that began to resemble a prize fight. Listless, I would stand flat-footed as he bounded around me for a layup, so he stopped bounding around me and started bounding into me.

You can only knock a seventeen-year-old down so many times before he reacts. When I did, bounding into him and taking up a hard shot, he would block it away like a horse tail flitting flies. By Wednesday I was mad enough to stop speaking to Coach in class. He just smiled. I would show him, I thought. I would beat him up if I had to.

I never did. The games got closer, and I made more shots. I played harder, determined to prove myself, but he won every game. When he knocked me down, he picked me up. When I knocked him down, I let him lay. By the end of our games, I was tired and mad. He had made me mad. I did not realize why, but I was mad, more at myself now than him.

"Keep shooting the ball." He walked by, spoke, and walked on.

Thursday night our game was closer. I shot the ball, five for thirteen, and missed a lot of easy shots. Again the team picked up the slack. By Friday I had resigned myself to doing my job on the boards and letting the others carry the scoring load. We were playing Snyder, and they could score points in bunches. It would be a tough game.

By halftime we were down six points, and I had gone two for eight. Our offense depended on opening up the inside by scoring from long range and alternating the ball generously to the open player. Snyder, having scouted us, had adjusted their defense, collapsing inside on our centers and forcing the outside shot. If we couldn't get the ball inside and couldn't hit from the outside, we were in a world of hurt.

I sat on the bench as our head coach went over a scheme to open up the game, always the tactician. We all knew it would not work. I wiped the beads of sweat off my face and arms with a soft towel then hung it veil-like over my head. Coach sat down beside me.

"Keep shooting the ball."

"I can't hit from outside! I haven't shot worth a darn since February." I was mad again. How could he expect me to shoot the ball, knowing how poorly I had played?

He looked me squarely in the face, almost startling me. I had not seen that look before. He was unsmiling, genuine, serious.

"You stop shooting, you don't score. You don't score, we can't win. Keep shooting the ball."

He knew something that I did not know, but the way he said those words caused me to understand that he knew. I didn't believe him. But I knew he knew.

The next time I saw his face, really saw his face, was with about sixty seconds left in the game. We had battled back in the second half. The defense had collapsed off of me and the point guard and left us open. We shot the ball, first me and then him, hitting long shot after long shot until the other team was forced to reconvene their original defense. Our middle opened up, and the game was won. The head coach replaced the starters with subs with a minute left, and as my sub entered, I shook his hand and walked to the bench. And I saw Coach's face.

One big, toothy, unadulterated, happy grin—for me. I sat down next to him on the bench and waited for the end to come. As the final second clicked off the clock, fans and players, now champions, celebrated on and off the floor. I put the towel over my head on the bench and cried silently. Coach, next to me on the bench, skipped the celebration, put his arm around my shoulder, and cried too.

In the locker room, around our District Champion trophy, we had our picture taken for the local paper. We would easily win our regional game the following Wednesday and travel to the state tournament a week later. I dressed slowly, somehow knowing that this moment would quickly pass, and I tried to savor it like a good steak. I did not know then that it would never pass, and I would be able to come back to it again and again, easily, like a trusted friend.

I went to the coach's office, where Coach was combing his prematurely thinning hair.

"Thanks, Coach," was all I said.

He nodded and smiled, and I knew then it was all he needed to hear.

He quit coaching that year. His dad had died, and he went back to help his mom and sister on the farm, giving up what he loved to help his family. He had a stroke a couple of years ago, and I hear he's not doing too well. I saw him at a reunion before the stroke, and he looked good.

I do not admit that I know much about coaching, and though I have coached a Little League team for a few years, I still have much to learn. I do know that much of what I try to instill when I coach is not my own invention, but borrowed, shamelessly, from Coach.

There was a time when Coach could have pounded my square peg into a round hole, but he held back, instead finding a square hole that fit me better. Even with that, he had to do some pounding.

If I have any advice on which I trust you can rely, it is this: Know your kids; find the hole into which they most easily fit; believe in them more than they believe in themselves. And when things are going as badly as can be imagined, sidle up to them and gently tell them, "Keep on shooting."

14

RASPBERRIES

People ask you for criticism, but they only want praise.
Somerset Maugham, *Of Human Bondage*

Hey big mouth, how do you spell *triple?*
**Shoeless Joe Jackson,
responding to a heckling Cleveland
fan, who kept asking the illiterate
Jackson if he could spell *illiterate,*
after hitting a triple**

It is a difficult task to make the distinction between criticism and compliment. We have tried to create a subclass of criticism that is somehow less offensive because its intent is to build rather than tear down, hence its moniker, "constructive criticism." The giver, of course, wants his comments to be taken as positive; he adjusts his comments' intent without adjusting their content. However, it is not the pitcher but the catcher who determines how the ball feels when caught.

Kids, for the most part, are mercilessly brutal in their discourse with one another. They have not yet learned the nuance of tact. They talk to and about each other like they mean it. But because they are naive to their own tenderness, their comments injure innocently and the wounds caused by their remarks heal easily. Only when the injury is inflicted with the rancor born of adult inflection do the words heal slowly, if at all.

When adults correct a child, we most generally do so with the gentle caress of a swinging ax. Our words, mere to us, are more significant to our children, having been issued from a mount higher than Olympus, the precipice of parenthood.

Parents are the main source of this overawed sense of importance, but any contact with children presents an opportunity to be either grasped or squandered. In Little League, your children and the children of others listen to what is said and to what is left unsaid, and they hear both what we want them to hear and what they hear because of our own shortcomings.

A coach, a parent, even a fan, must weigh the delicate balance between criticism and compliment. It is good and right to teach our children what we know. But it is not teaching, in the purest sense of the word, if we do not expect them to learn. Teaching offered for less than that is a sham on our children's time.

I offer no special rules. Here, as most anywhere else, few things are black and white. I can only offer my experience, my mistakes and my successes, as a guide into the foggy wandering of right and wrong. Yogi Berra once said, "When you come to a fork in the road, take it." Little better advice can I offer than that. I would advise you, though, to remember the road once taken, and if you happen upon a dead end, mark it on your map so you don't take it again.

A problem with raspberries—baseball jargon for critical comments of disapproval—is that they are more often than not made openly and publicly. Therefore, they cannot be first shielded from public consumption by close quarters or quiet reflection. And in Little League, such public consumption harms.

One of the all-time greatest sporting achievements was the Olympic hockey team championships of 1980 at Lake Placid. I watched the USA versus USSR on a tape delay with a few of my buddies in law school, successfully avoiding the knowledge of its outcome, so that while the game had long since been decided, we watched it as if it were live over barbecued ribs, cold drinks, and anticipation. A year or so later, as Hollywood is wont to do, a made-for-TV movie attempting to re-create the excitement of the original event was made about the team, its coach Herb Brooks, and the Olympic experience.

A scene from the movie, which is authentic according to the participants, dealt with Coach Brooks and his team captain, Mike Eruzione, and their relationship on and off the ice. The team was young and sensitive, and Brooks was not a gentle man. His technique of singling out individual players for criticism was hurting the team morale and the players' confidence. He knew his captain could take it, but he was not sure about the others. Brooks devised a plan that was simple genius.

"Mike," he said, in the locker room after a practice, "when I am yelling at the whole team, I'll yell at you, but I'll call you 'Eruzione,' so you'll know it's the team I'm upset with. You're the captain; they'll take criticism from you better than me. I yell at you; you yell at them. When I am yelling at you and you alone, I'll call you 'Mike.' "

So was born a plan that deferred the direct anger of Coach Brooks from the individual players who were not yet prepared for it, yet provided the clear hand of disciplined instruction for those players who needed it. The team went on to beat the Russians, impossibly, and then to beat Finland one cold Sunday morning to win the gold medal. It is a memory deeply etched in my mind.

Parents want their children to play ball; and they want their children to play well. Children want to play ball; and they want to play well. This unison of purpose ought to produce symmetry but often does not. Playing well for one is not playing ball well for another. Unless we are willing to invest as much effort in our children off the playing field as is needed to achieve our joint goals, we must leave our criticism in the box. This baseball is not an easy game.

I can't recall where we were playing, but I know that we were not at home. The team we faced was a machine, precise and automatic. Their coaches barked out instructions like twin Dobermans—fierce and demanding. Their boys responded with exactitude. Their ins and outs from the field looked like wind sprints, ours like jogs in the park. Their coaches were determined to win, and their secret to winning, though hardly hidden, was perfect execution. Their boys looked and acted older than twelve-year-olds. At first.

Our boys, on the other hand, looked and acted every bit their age. We balanced the opposing team's assembly-line perfection with our Rube Goldberg contraption. We offset their Patton-like drills with whimsical disinterest. Their boys eschewed playful conviviality; ours embraced it. It should have been a blitzkrieg against the Slovac army, but we stayed loose and close, trailing by only two after five innings. We were ahead in laughs.

It wasn't that our boys didn't want to win—they did. It was simply that the other team's coaches wanted to win more than their boys, and that had spilled over, toxically, into the stands where their fans sat. No play, however well played, was played well enough; no hit, far enough. No out was out enough for their insatiable fans, as they sat watching their children, demanding correction.

Their downfall started quietly. Most disasters do. A slight shift of the earth. A passed ball. A hot grounder—too hot to handle. A dropped popped fly. A walk, a clean hit, then another. The kind of thing you might expect from a team of twelve-year-olds—but never from a machine.

The coaches, used to perfection, grew irate at this miscalculated play, singling out the cogs and pulleys that seemed out of time. They yelled rules and instructions. Fans, less articulate and less disciplined, just yelled. It would have been more effective to wail at the moon.

Their boys knew they had made a mistake, committed an error, dropped a fly. The oratory of Demosthenes won't put the ball back into the glove after it's hit the ground. "You shouldn't have been speeding," after the ticket's been issued, is the adult equivalent of "You should've caught the ball," when it lies naked in front of a young boy on the ground. Neither say much for our advanced powers of observation. Some people, perhaps out of their own inadequacy, perhaps out of a sense of despair because of lost control, find no other way to express themselves. These coaches and fans were those people.

Little League ought to be a chance to learn the best from the best. It is also a chance to learn the worst. Life and baseball are alike in many ways. Not all is good; not all is bad. Yet there was a feeling I had that day, an unmistakable embarrassment for my age, that left me hollow and discouraged.

After we won the game and our opponent's humiliation was complete, not by our hands but by their own, our boys left the field, happy, yet strangely silent after a win. There was little rejoicing, as if they somehow sensed how it feels for a newborn to be eaten by its parent.

How do you turn boys into men? At what point should gentle correction step aside for tough instruction? When is "nice try" a weak excuse for "try harder"? When is effort not enough? These questions and more raced through my mind late into the night after that game. How can you balance the rigors and demands of baseball with the innocence of a twelve-year-old Little Leaguer? When does a gentle push become a shove?

I sat outside, under the open sky, dark now, and spit generously with sparkles marking different suns of different worlds, innumerable. I could count them, as high as numbers go, but daylight would first intercede, and lighten the sky, making the counting impossible. And I could start over the next night, until infinity dragged me into its perilous well. I could learn the answer if I had enough time, but I would never have enough time. The best you can do is the best you can do.

I heard the screen door open. Chad appeared from around the side of the house, a cold tea in his hand. He offered it to me and sat down.

"Thanks," I said.

He looked up with me, up into the vastness, bigger than big, unending, ongoing, observable, and hidden. All the answers lay out there, waiting. Times like these are apparitions, fleeting, coming unaware. Later they slink back, a ghost, to haunt you. They grow old and away, like your child, until you wish them to be more than they are, yet know them to be less than they were.

"How many stars are there, Dad?"

"I don't know." A pause.

"Think anyone knows?"

"I s'pose somebody knows."

"How do you s'pose he knows?"

"I reckon he just knows or counted 'em or just guessed." Still looking up, I sipped from my tea.

"I s'pose it's okay to guess on somethin' like that."

No harm in that, I thought. Who could complain. If you guessed and were off a million or so, well, who would complain. Just adjust the number and move on to the next contestant. It's okay to guess with stars. They are numerous, anonymous, and far away.

"Chad." I turned to him. "What did you think of the game?"

"It was okay."

"You won." As if that were the determining end point on the straight line of success.

"I kinda wished we'd've lost. Then maybe the fans wouldn'ta been so hard on their players."

"You noticed?" I asked, wondering how much.

"Yeah," he half-laughed out loud, sarcastic, even at twelve. "It wasn't much fun playing today, even though we won. I kept thinkin' I was glad I wasn't them."

No revelation there, just simple resolve. The changes from boy to man happen like that, a slow wash of the Mississippi of experience and emotion eating away the bank, changing the course, out, then back in its boundaries. The truth is that you never really know. You never really know when it is that a boy becomes a man, when you can begin to put the edge on your comment and sharpen its effect.

The answer to this riddle, while impossible to discover, should not be unsought. Simply because you can't know the answer does not mean you should not seek it. In seeking it, you will watch the flow of that river, watch the change in the boundaries, and discover at the dawn of one morning indescribably similar to all those other mornings that came and went before it, that it is not the same, nor will it be ever again. You will not know the time of the change, but be assured that if you fail to watch, you will most assuredly fail to see.

In the tumult that stretches from boy into man, you will find yourself and your child alone together. And you will know what to say and how to say it to a young man not quite ready to listen but desperately eager to hear. There is no more fertile soil than that of a young mind in innocence, and no field so badly abused by poor husbandry.

Temper your tongues. Treat your Little Leaguers to the respect of a private word when a public one would do damage. Remember the waters flow by but once, and though these kids may look and act older than twelve, they are not. Wish not upon them an age where precision in execution is demanded of them before they demand it of themselves.

Let your children grow up with their games, and let them hold fast to their youth that is too soon gone and forgotten. Let the stars teach us that they need not be counted to know that they still possess a beauty and mystery that stirs the souls of those who would look to them on a quiet summer's eve and wonder if not knowing all the answers diminishes the search for the truth.

15

HUMBATTABATTAHUM

I am sorry when any language is lost, because languages are the pedigree of nations.

Samuel Johnson

The bases were drunk, and I painted the black with my best yakker. But blue squeezed me, and I went full. I came back with my heater, but the stick flares one the other way and chalk flies for two bases. Three earnies! Next thing I know, skipper hooks me and I'm sipping suds with the clubby.

Ed Lynch, New York Mets pitcher

Besides offering up memories and experiences wrought from dirt and mud, precious and coveted, like Ming pottery from ancient China, baseball in its infinite generosity has also given us a language of its own—a neat yet uneven language, Faulkner-esque, babbled about the infields of America by children who understand what it means. It is a language where syllables, semicolons, and commas are cast aside as obstinate obstructions to the musical flow of guttural utterances strung together in a chorus of enthusiasm. This language is not foreign—it is more domestic than the King's English.

Interestingly, as babies, the children who now speak this language fluently, once spoke its ancestral language. A first "da" becomes soon enough, "dadda," and after much encouragement ultimately culminates into a clearer "daddy." Conversely, now, "batter" becomes "batta," and finally, the strangely poetic "battabatta."

We adults, while ignoring the lyric, have nonetheless appropriated baseball idiom to use in our other lives. I recall one day, or maybe it was several spliced together, that illustrates the point I am attempting to make. Perhaps I should let it be made without any interference.

Dark overcast skies threatened the reign of the midday sun, crowding it back into the dimness, making the day dreary. The field was full. Boys hovered near their assigned positions as the dugouts carelessly spilled others out of their openings. The game was in progress, and fans sat mingled together in uncertain order, watching the action and commenting on the state of affairs. One and then another would stand up and amble down the concrete bleacher steps and over to the stand for a cool drink or a hot dog.

"Humbattabattahum-humbattabattahum." The catcher droned his hypnotic words, then at the last instant before the ball struck his pud, shouted "Swing!" seeking to mesmerize the batter into an attempt at a poor pitch.

"Rock 'n fire, buddy. C'mon now rock 'n fire," the infield yelled to the pitcher.

"Nosticknostick. Battabatta, nostick."

The pitch was thrown and called ball. The batter was immobile.

"Awww, look good, Blue. Right aw'cross. Pitchit, now, buddy, rock 'n fire, same place now," said one.

"Lookerlookerrr. No stick. He's looking for a free riiide," said another. "Chuckerinthere, buddy."

"Steeeriiike threeee!" shouted Blue.

"Awww, Champy, ya gotta swing the stick. Can't hit 'er watchin'. Gotta swing the stick." The boy walked back to the dugout.

By the stand two men—one dressed in Key overalls and wearing a seed corn hat on his mostly bald farmer-tanned head, and the other wearing jeans, boots, and a plaid shirt—stood eating hot dogs. Overalls looked up at the threatening overcast sky.

"Looks like rain."

Jeans, biting off a hunk of dog, paused, chewed it into the side of his mouth, then answered, "Don't think so. Probably pass north again. Could use a good soaking."

"They been blamin' that El Niño for everything happened the last two years."

"Yeah, must be somethin' to it."

"I think the weatherman's out in left field," said Jeans, washing his dog down with a swallow from his icy drink.

Out in left field, a boy, bored with inactivity, had taken to watching the clover, glancing up at the game before him and then down again to the clump that intruded into the grassed outfield expanse. He had never found a four-leaf clover.

Suddenly a sharp crack sent his eyes upward, searching for the white sphere in the cloud. It was heading his way. Frantic, he ran in, then adjusting quickly to its arc, saw that it was going to go over his head. He stopped sharply and reversed directions, running backward, his glove outstretched and over his shoulder. The clover would wait.

"Attaboy, attaboy, nice poke!" The dugout chorus shouted at the batter, now base runner, rounding first. "Gonna go a mile. Smokin' poke, big hit, gonna be a big inning!"

Counterparts encouraged the left fielder.

"C'mon now, underrrit, over yer head, move on it! Let's go, Rickeee; make a plaaaay!"

Rickey raced heavily back, angry at the clover.

"Keep haulin', Rickeee, under it now," shouted help from center field.

"C'mon now, round the bags, never catch it, gonna go over his head." The third-base coach was waving the runner over to third. The ball was coming down now, Rickey still on a dead run backward, focused. Outstretched, his glove on the end of his hand, reaching upward, the ball landed in the end of the webbing.

"Oooouuuuttt!" signaled Blue.

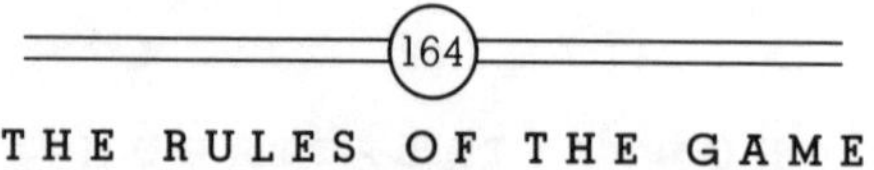

"Awww! Look what I found! Lucky dawg. We wuz robbed. Nowaynoway!"

"AhrighttRickeeee! What a catch! Did ya see that? Way to go, Rickeeee!"

Up in the stands the fans applauded both for the hit that wasn't and the catch that was.

Two women, off and on interested in the play on the field, began to talk again about other things. One, wearing jean shorts and a red blouse, sat cross-legged, her hand on her chin. The other, shorter, with straight blonde hair pulled back in a ponytail, leaned lazily against the backrest.

"Need anything Friday night?" asked Jean Shorts.

"I don't think so, unless you've got extra paper plates." Ponytail looked in. "I've only got about two packages."

"How many're coming?"

"Ballpark figure: about a hundred."

"I'll bring what we've got over tonight. It should be enough." And on it went into the late innings, on the field and off, the language interwoven into the culture.

Players learn to speak by imitation—by hearing others and speaking like them. The words flow easily into one another, and tone and inflection become paramount, altering meaning and emphasis. Adults, just as easily, borrow a phrase from the lexicon of the game, insert it like a spark plug into the engine of a conversation, and hum merrily along. Baseball is richer when it lends itself.

Yet below the surface of the easily observed, something deeper happens when young children learn a language and adults adopt phrases from that language. To learn that your counterpart speaks the same language, especially a language as comfortable and familiar as a worn flannel shirt, opens ears and minds. The commonality of understanding from the language, the *baseballspeak,* bridges a gap created by age and stature.

It is often an insignificant wind that signals a change in the weather. At first a soft south breeze brings the heat and wet air, creating billowing clouds of white and black, churning upward thousands of feet until, finally, moisture rains down on the earth below. So it is with the opening refrain of a common language between parent and child.

My daughter, now dusty and dirty, sweat beaded below the bill of her ball cap, walked over to the truck, glove in hand. The game, now ended, had not gone well.

Mandi is thin, tallish, and quick. She got her mother's legs and her grandma's disposition. Her competitive spirit comes partly from me but mostly from her brother, who competes with her at every opportunity. They race from church to the car, fight over the front seat, shoot baskets in the front drive—best two out of three, then three out of five, and on and on until one or the other gives up from fatigue. They fight over drumsticks when the fried chicken is plentiful and over affection when it isn't. With one another, life is one big contest. Chad, older, bigger, and more experienced, usually wins, but Mandi, growing into herself, comes closer and closer and wins often enough to satisfy.

Ten-year-old girls playing softball want to win as badly as Little Leaguers playing a different game. There is no drop-off in incentive,

no lapse in intensity. Girls, perhaps not as conditioned to the art of hiding emotions, play their game with similar desire, only more openly, wounding more easily when the ball bounces awry. Mandi takes her softball to heart, and when her team disappoints, she shows it like a big screen TV.

She got into the truck with me, and we backed out into the street and onto the highway, homeward. She was silent as I stopped for sodas. She said nothing until her soda was across her lips and down her dry throat. Her glove lay at her feet on the floorboard, where she kicked it in controlled disgust.

"Mandi, that was a tough one to lose."

"It was my fault," she said, near tears.

"You can't blame yourself," I answered, but I knew what she meant. She had let one go through her legs in the next to last inning, and the tying run scored. She had struck out in the last inning, and she felt responsible for the outcome. "No one player can win or lose any game."

Repeat that a hundred times after a ball goes through your legs, and see if it makes you a believer.

"But if I had caught it, they wouldn'ta scored, and we'd'a won." The simple logic of a child.

"Maybe. Maybe not. If you hadn't gotten your hit early, your team wouldn't have scored the runs it did. Did you play your hardest?"

"I tried to," she said, softening, questioning.

Did she expect me to answer that question? "Did you do your best?"

"I shouldn't'a struck out," she countered, not convinced.

"Why not?" I paused, took a sip from my pop, and steered, lights like open eyes on the blacktop ahead.

"'Cause I should'a hit it." She put her pop down now, wondering where I was headed.

"Did you do everything you were supposed to do?" She had practiced batting every day since the season started—in the front yard with her brother.

"Yup. I watched the ball, had my bat ready, choked up, and I swung it level." Remembering the at bat, she had it in her mind and replayed it again painfully. "I did everything."

"Then you shouldn't feel bad."

She paused, took another sip from the can, and set the can between her legs on the seat. The windows were down, the warm freshness of the summer breeze blowing into the truck. Her hair tossed up and about.

"How come I didn't hit it? I did everything you told me to do. How come I didn't hit it?"

She was right. We had practiced. Her form and swing were even and fair. Her stance exact. She had followed every instruction to a T and had come up empty. Her question did not stop at the unsuccessful at bat, and as much as I thought it okay to dodge it, I could not. She was asking me simply how she could do all that was asked of her by her father—formerly infallible, as fathers are in their daughters' eyes—and find, starkly, that it was not enough. She was asking me in the only language she understood about trust and what to do with it tomorrow.

"Did I ever tell you," I answered, slowing down now, careful not

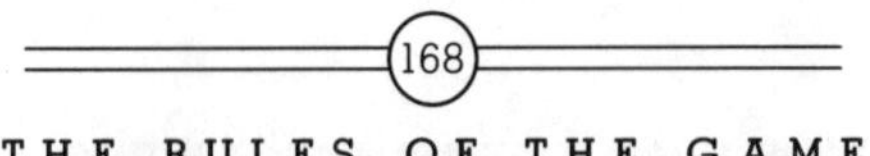

to miss the turnoff, "that you would hit it every time if you did everything right?"

"No." I hadn't, but what was the point of doing everything right if you didn't hit it every time?

"Sometimes in baseball you can do everything right, and it still isn't enough. You can swing right, and it still isn't enough. You can swing the bat like you're told and still miss the ball. That is the way it is in baseball."

"So, even if I do my best, it still might not be enough."

"No." I turned onto the graveled county road. "If you do your best, it's always enough."

"But I still might strike out."

"Right. But if you do your best, even that's enough."

Her puzzlement drifted into silence as we drove the rest of the route home. I could not be sure she had understood me; she did not ask me to explain it again, so I guessed that she either understood or was confused enough to give it a rest.

I had hoped to explain to her—although I was not sure then that I believed it myself—that in the effort was the glory, and the result, too often glorified, was mere by-product.

I tried to explain in the language we both understood. Perhaps she had learned this lesson. Perhaps she would learn it in another way. For now, it was the best I could do to explain it as I had and hope that she had understood.

16

SIGNS AND SIGNALS

He answered and said to them, "When it is evening, you say, 'It will be fair weather, for the sky is red.' And in the morning, 'There will be a storm today, for the sky is red and threatening.' Do you know how to discern the appearance of the sky, but cannot discern the signs of the times?"
Matthew 16:2–3

If I'm looking at you, you're hitting . . . If I'm walking away from you and spitting, you're hitting . . . If I'm looking at you and spitting, you're not hitting . . . If I'm walking away and not spitting, you're not hitting.

Casey Stengel, giving signs to Dodger Frank Skaff, who added, "Those are exactly what his signs were. I'll never forget them. They give you an idea why some of the guys were missing them."

Part of the artistry in baseball is a duplicitous deception practiced by one team on another. Once Little Leaguers understand that, they're yours forever. Children love to play secret tricks on one another, and baseball, played properly, is at one level open, honest, and sincere, and on another, secretive, deceptive, and hidden. The simple object is to pass messages from coaches to players without the opposing team discerning the message. After that, nothing about it is simple.

At the professional level, signs and signals are more intricate and complicated and can change even during the playing of a game. Almost as much stock is placed in stealing signals as in receiving them, hence the added complexity.

Little Leaguers, however, preoccupied with tasks like hitting and catching—barely surmountable efforts in themselves—cannot be troubled with too much thinking. It is necessary to keep the signs simple and direct yet still hidden from others.

We used a method, a pattern, which I wonder if I should divulge since it has been in use for years, and my writing about it would simply tip off opponents in the games still to be played in the seasons ahead. Perhaps even the tried and true ought to be changed now and then. Three signals. First, any touching of the skin—face, arm, or hands—signified steal. Skin equals steal. Second, a swipe of the belt meant bunt. Belt equals bunt. Third, when we wanted the batter to take a pitch, generally to allow a base runner an unimpeded opportunity to steal, a swipe across the chest was signaled.

The only variable from game to game was the all-important indicator—the extra sign that told the boys "this is not a drill." The first sign after the indicator was for real, all else was balderdash. In one game, a touch of the bill of the hat might be the indicator. Chest, belt, skin, hat, belt, skin equaled bunt and nothing else. In the next game, taking the hat completely off the head might be the indicator, or scratching your nose, or pulling your ear, or clapping your hands. The beauty of this method was that the boys had to remember only three signs and the indicator and then recall which sign came first after the indicator. Simple.

A missed sign, where a boy does not execute upon a coach's order, cuts like a dull knife. The main reason for this is that in the back, or perhaps the front, of the coach's mind, he feels his signals actually are important to the ebb and flow of the game. This is understandable. What else during the play does he have? This is the only control a coach has over his players once play starts; therefore, if it is meaningless, so is he. This cannot be. A missed sign, therefore, is either an intentional, or more likely, a confused lost opportunity to control in some way that which is, for all intents and purposes, probably beyond control anyway. (Telling a coach that is akin to telling the inventor of the traffic light that he could have left yellow out.)

With more experienced players, you might occasionally develop additional, more complex, signs–sort of an advanced algebra for the better students. Squeeze plays, double steals, pickoff plays, pitch-outs–all of these require something special and different from those signs just described. With each layer of intricacy comes a new complexity and opportunity for failure. But there also comes a melding of thought and action, for nonverbal communication does demand mental quickness, and when thought coerces action, baseball separates itself from other sports less cerebral.

This is why, I think, George Will, veteran thinker, writes about baseball and why he lambastes those who call the game languid and leisurely. Will, like the players, uses his time between pitches to observe the mental cornucopia that lies like a feast on the field before him; others are satisfied with another handful of buttered popcorn.

I disagree with Will only in the sense that he excludes the concept of leisure with exercised thinking. I do not. The level of the game about which I write is not major but Little League. I wonder, however, if it is not as likely that Wade Boggs, kicking the dirt in front of him between a 3–2 count and a strikeout, is thinking about home, and later, and tomorrow, just as the Little Leaguer does on a smaller scale.

Signs and signals, designed to guide us silently into better things—into advantage and chance—can act as benchmarks on a path leading longingly left down a wrong turn, into a dead end. Backtracking, we always spot them, big as day. Embarrassed, we ruefully acknowledge that, yes, it must have been there all along, but, no, we didn't see it, and, no, we can't say why. It is easier, once you have become lost and found your way back, to admit it than accept that you did not know where you were going in the first place.

Every June in Omaha, the best college baseball teams come, gathered together under the bright, hot Nebraska sun, for the world series of college baseball, at the conclusion of which one team is crowned national champion. Many players, stars in their own right, go on to sign major league contracts and play successfully in the bigs. For two weeks, they are but aspirations, unknown, hopeful, uncertain of fulfillment, going on or going home.

A few years back, we rented a bus, bought some bleacher tickets, and took our kids to Omaha to watch a Sunday doubleheader on the first weekend of competition. We boarded the bus—one of those sleek, dark-windowed gliders you used to see in Greyhound commercials—in front of the high school, early Sunday morning, for the ninety-minute drive to Omaha. Endless chatter hummed as the tires milked the miles out of the blacktop. Time droned on until a highway billboard on the outskirts of Omaha welcomed us to the home of the college world series.

The bus groaned up the steep hill next to Rosenblatt Stadium, circled around and then into a long row of other buses, parked, and unloaded a mixture of kids and adults, boys and girls. Rosenblatt was at that time a typical small ballpark, home of the Omaha Royals, the Kansas City triple-A farm club. It is cozy and you can spit peanut shells from third row almost to the bull pen rubber. During the players' warm-up, you can hear them razz and banter as you eavesdrop, permissibly, on their talk. There are no seats too far from the field to be involved in the action.

Rosenblatt is a delight. Every child should go to a ballpark like this with his or her mom or dad. They will learn that baseball is not always about money and publicity, and that young players not yet good enough to be spoiled by their own excess still strive to achieve for the sake of their own desire.

We had a block of seats stretching upward from the first row, even with first base and moving out to right field. The adults gathered in their seats, mindful of duty. The kids explored and wandered, talking to ballplayers who paid attention, buying, and eating, mindful of nothing. It was as it should be.

Two older fellows, experienced series watchers, sat across an aisle from me, eating popcorn and drinking Coke. The older one wore a Cubs ball cap, set back on his head, and a gray tuft of curls billowed out from either side. The other, too old to be his son, but still younger, wore a short-sleeve shirt with suspenders. His eyes sparkled behind a pair of gold and shiny wire-rimmed glasses. They talked loud enough to overhear if you strained, but not disturbingly so.

"Pitchin' wins these games," said the older one, popcorn in hand.

"Agreed. But here, one swing with the wind can turn it around mighty quick," said the other, sipping his soda.

"A lot of three-run homers here."

"Yeah, and you know what ol' Earl Weaver said about that."

"Yup." But no clue was divulged.

They would comment on averages, pitchers, the future prospects of a team's star, but they seemed content to let the game pass by without much real passion. It was the second bill of the doubleheader they had come to see, and their anticipation whetted mine.

The second game started on time, about five-thirty in the afternoon, and would eventually stretch into the evening darkness. Mississippi State was playing Stanford. Each team had one loss. The loser of this double-elimination tournament would go home, and the winner would advance on in the loser's bracket with a chance, a long shot to be sure, at the finals.

Among many good ballplayers, one stood out: Bobby Thigpen, who played center field and occasionally pitched for Mississippi State. No one knew then what he would become, but the sages next to me had an inkling.

"Good-looking prospect," said Cubbie, pointing his half-empty beer in Thigpen's direction. "Throws like hot honey."

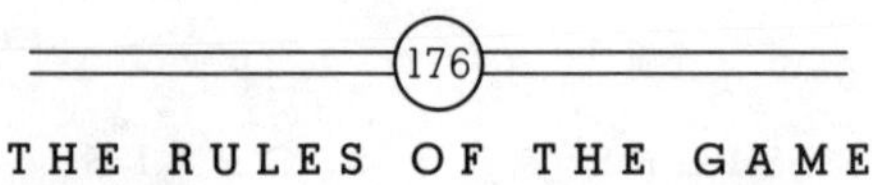

"Going places. Draft's next week." Suspenders had concentrated now on Thigpen warming up in center.

"Class of the bunch. No doubt."

My eyes and the eyes of those around me were now drawn to Thigpen. He could float a ball effortlessly on a line to second from center, and he moved with the ease of youth, agile and facile in the outfield.

The late-afternoon June sun over the southern bleachers raked the sweat out of us. Finally shedding our shirts—still okay among the natives—we cooled slightly with the gentle, intermittent breeze that wafted in from the southern sky. The ball game was into the third inning before the sun had moved behind the man-made horizon. We replaced our shirts on burnt backs and arms that felt good, like hot, sweaty saddle leather after a trail ride. The lights were on, and the game was knotted after three.

Thigpen was doing it all: hitting and fielding. He threw behind a runner rounding second on a short line drive and dusted him. His efforts alone looked to be enough to keep his team in the game.

In the bottom of the eighth, Stanford had the bases full with two out. The Mississippi State pitcher looked tired having given up long flies on the last two bats. With two outs, the coach left him in since he was the ace of the staff.

The next batter struck a mighty blow that looked gone, solidly struck to deep center field. Thigpen shot back, eyeing the ball over his right shoulder as he ran headlong toward the warning track and fence, 425 feet from home. The ball was coming down, but on an arc that created a sure collision with the fence, yet Thigpen, now on the warning track, did not slow down. He crashed hard into the fence as the ball hit his glove, knocking him back onto the middle of the warning track, head over heels. He lay motionless and hurt. He paused momentarily, and then he held his gloved arm up, the ball safely secured.

"Oh my goodness! What a catch!" shouted Cubbie, his hat off the back of his head as he rose in excitement.

The crowd cheered unanimously. Few of our kids had ever seen a catch like that, or ever would for that matter. Thigpen had made it right in front of their eyes. Surely the game was his.

The top of the ninth saw Thigpen's team add two runs. Thigpen garnered a single, moving a runner over, and they went back on the field, up by two, with three outs to play. The pitcher, shaky last inning but now rejuvenated, stayed in.

Sometimes the signs are obvious and can't be missed. Other times they are not. People watch and see them differently; no two sets of eyes see them the same. The pitcher looked strong, but he was finished. He struggled getting the first out, loaded the bases, and managed the second out on a short fly that held the base runners–but by then the flashing red light of "enough" glared across all of Rosenblatt. The skipper motioned to center. How fitting–Thigpen would relieve the game he had almost single-handedly won. Nothing better than throwing the final out as a relief pitcher could top his perfect day. He jogged in from center, changed gloves, and took his warm-up pitches.

One pitch later, a blazing fastball down the center of the plate, it was all over. The ball sailed over the fence in left center, and the home run ended the hopes of Mississippi State and the dreams of Bobby Thigpen. He had been directly responsible for both winning and losing the game. But as always, it's what you eat last that stays in your mouth. In a matter of minutes, high exaltation turned sour. Now nothing but a bad memory of one mistake made in the open glare of the watching world.

This was a lesson I thought that taught itself. Yet all the clichés and hackneyed sportswriting in the next day's paper did not do justice to what had happened. The general sense was that Thigpen had gone from hero to goat and that maybe he'd survive. I saw it a little differently.

Bobby Thigpen neither won nor lost that game in Omaha that Sunday. If he fell at all, it was only from a falsely erected high manufactured by our own unrealistic expectations of him. He could only do what he could do. His signals to us, the throw, the catch, meant only that and nothing more. He didn't throw a strikeout, probably lucky for him, because his trip to the big leagues, where he plays now, would have inevitably been downhill. It is not much fun to go downhill from a highlight.

Along the paths we travel we meet and pass expectations both of our own making and those made by others. We are given signs or signals, which open our eyes to a smoother road, a better way. We often eschew the easy path, recognizing it as a dead end or a wrong road, easy but leading nowhere we want to go. Other times, perhaps wearied by our constant searching, we take the road most inviting, smooth, and straight, ignoring the signs marking its dangers.

No one can say why until after it occurs, and even then it's only a guess. Why does a young boy learning the game miss a take sign and swing at a bad pitch? Why does a coach, seeing his pitcher weary, convince himself beyond reason that there is yet another inning left in his arm gone limp? Why do we enjoy the surprise of a heroic catch, then lament the catcher when the surprises evaporate into the usual and ordinary? What is it that causes us to expect excellence, demand it, and just as readily, delight in the failure to excel?

When I coach the boys of Little League, I give them a sign and expect it to be followed. What then can be said if I, when given a sign, fail to understand it and follow it myself? Signs will be missed, signals will go unheeded, and plays accordingly will be fouled up. And the inexorable, unending march toward the end will not go smoothly. We, having failed along the way to do that which is expected of us, are caught unawares by the complicity of our own satisfaction. Even then, the mistake is rarely fatal.

17

SAFE AT HOME

The somber comfort, all the peace which springs,
From the large aggregate of little things;
On these small cares of daughter, wife or friend,
The almost sacred joys of home depend.

Hannah More, "Sensibility"

Now more than ever, we need a change of pace in baseball. Ballparks should be happy places. They should always smell like freshly cut grass.

Bill Veeck

He danced off third base toward home, off, then back, tentative and caustic. Sixty feet away, flat on the ground, lay the hard rubber geometric that beckoned him, elusive and inviting. He was the winning run. A throw to third caught him leaning toward adulation, and he had to dive headlong back to the bag to save himself.

"Safe," signaled the umpire, then "Time," as the boy lifted up off the ground and raised his hand.

That was close, he thought, as his coach told him all the obvious. He listened but did not hear, focused on his own mission. Again, dancing, the boy balanced on the balls of his feet. His eyes met the pitcher's, who burned back a glare, glancing away to the catcher and then back again, nervous and wary.

The pitcher started his windup, and the boy advanced concurrent with his movement. A smallish boy in the box waited, determined and stoic, chin set against the defense; his fists clenched on the cocked bat. The ball sailed hard and low out of the pitcher's hand, and the bat swung quickly, downward, topping the ball toward third base.

Reacting to the crack of the bat, the dancing boy darted home. The ball skipped to his left, meeting and then passing him like a car on a highway. Instinctively, he knew the ball was coming home behind him, and the play would be close.

The third baseman, activated by the antics of the runner, moved down into a fielder's crouch as the ball spun and short-hopped toward him and into his glove. Shouts from the bench called out.

"Down! Down!" to the base runner.

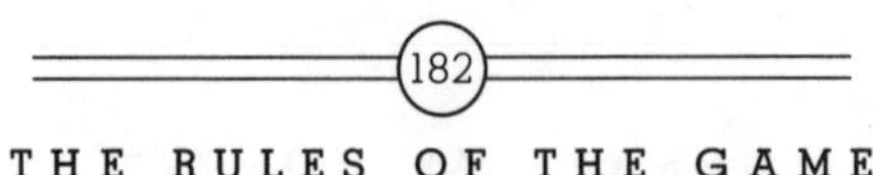

"Home! Home!" to the fielder. Nothing else needed to be said.

The fielder pulled the ball out of his glove and reared back, shifted his feet, and threw it home as the catcher, flipping off his mask, maneuvered into the base path between home and the oncoming runner.

Running upright, then lower, into a crouch, the runner flattened headlong into a slide, dirt and dust stirring, hopeful arms and hands reaching for safety. The ball thudded into the pud, and almost at the same time the tag went hard to the ground between the catcher's legs, onto the body.

Time froze in that instant as the fingers stretched and reached Sistine-like for the hard rubber plate.

"Safe! Safe! Safe!" Blue, arms horizontal again and again, ended the game. The bench of boys cleared in exultation, and the runner jumped up, dusted himself off, and welcomed the team. Congratulations all around, and they bumped and chortled happily back to the dugout—winners.

Reaching home safely happens countless times during a ball season. Events less dramatic occur in every game, inning upon inning to player after player. Even when the run is not as dramatic or as important, to the boy crossing home safely, it is always special. It is a mixture of feelings, perhaps so interwoven as to be indescribable. Accomplishment, success, safety. Reaching home safely means that a ballplayer has, through his own effort, successfully achieved the ultimate offensive goal of the game: Get on base and advance safely around them all until you score a run for your team.

It also means a time to gather yourself, rest from the immediate

rigors of the game, and enjoy the moment of success with your friends and teammates. Few times in a game offer as much opportunity to recount immediate success—always a favorite topic—as the time between a successful score and your next chance at the plate or in the field. Boys sit and wipe themselves off, dust and glory, onto the rapt attention of other boys waiting and hoping and dying to be in their place. The hit, the steal, the slide, the score are now blended like the elements of style in a short story filled with joy, wonder, and confidence. Few tell them better than the boys of Little League.

Watching a game last summer, it occurred to me at a quiet interlude between plays that the full meaning of the scoring moment is both stark and rich. On the active field of baseball, there is no place you are truly safe except at home. Everywhere else—every position and every base—poses a risk. On defense, there is no refuge. You are always susceptible to open failure, exposed by the very extroversion of the game. On offense, too, you stand similarly exposed, except at home. Even at first, second, and third, if you are successful reaching them, they offer only transient respite and protection.

At each base you do not control your advance. A new runner, pushing offensively from your rear, can move you off the base whether you want to advance or not. Every base, square and white, offers safe haven only if connected, and a momentary lapse in connection can be fatal. Delicately they cling to the bag, an occupier, realizing their stay is temporary and their welcome incomplete.

Only at home are you completely safe. Once there, you can dance off without fear, do a jig if you wish. No one can push you off once you're there, and the evolution of the hit reaches fruition. A run cannot advance beyond home. Safe at home means rest without fear, complete success in your grasp, and results realized. It is a good feeling.

We adults could learn a lesson from our Little League sons' and daughters' vigorous efforts to reach home plate. Ask them, away from the instant success of the score, if reaching home is easy. If they think carefully about the effort they expend in that accomplishment, they will tell you: No.

All the effort is compressed and almost forgotten in the consistently sought-after conclusion of reaching home and scoring a run. But the intricate, repetitive, and incessant groundwork of practice must first be laid. Years of developing beginning skills—holding a bat, timing a pitch, remembering a stance—all are essential to even a modest chance at success.

Swinging, timing, running, alertness, courage, speed, and cunning—the trip from batting to home plate is precarious, filled with pitfalls, and surrounded with failure. Advancing from base to base, while a lonely enterprise, often depends on the skill of others; it is a team effort. Faith in what those others do has as much to do with the success of that endeavor as your own skill.

Nothing in baseball can salvage the deflation of a boy's enthusiasm, who, standing on second after his own solid hit, is stranded through no fault of his own. Each singular effort in Little League, savored by the individual ego, is wasted unless followed by additional effort of teammates. The game accents the individual and alternately stresses the importance of team effort, without which the individual effort dies, languished on first, second, or third.

And so it is in our homes. The effort required to make and keep a safe and sound home for children is in its own way similarly prac-

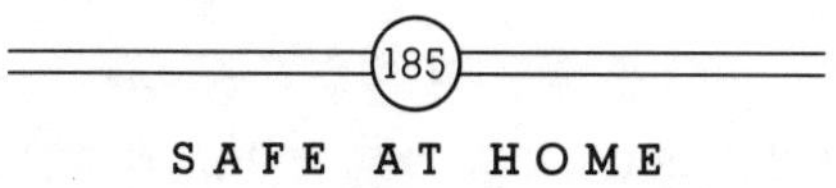

ticed. Just as young Little Leaguers do not come to the game blessed with the essential skills, neither do we parents inherit the skills we need to make and keep a home. Parenting, like pitching, is a practiced art. Only with and through judgment honed by experience does a parent learn to throw strikes and field the hard hoppers our children hit back at us. Some parents tire after a few innings and give up. Some parents are specialty players, relief pitchers capable of a few strong innings but no more. Only the specially motivated can go the distance. Baseball is an endless game, and commitment to the perpetuity of it is hard sacrifice, for you do not know, nor can you be assured, that the sacrifice will bring anything that resembles reward.

Often, like our children, we are defeated and discouraged. Often, like our children, we swing and miss, lose it in the sun, or let the easy grounder skid between our legs. Often, like our children, our effort is halfhearted, encumbered by nether thoughts that rise up into our lives and obstruct our vision and goals. Often, like our children, we simply fail, having given our best effort and learning that occasionally even our best is not enough to succeed.

We know (don't we?) that the game is endless. Our effort, then, must be endless also, lest we stop our work before the job is finished. But our job is never finished, and therein lies the quandary. Who, knowing the obligation involved, would readily undertake it?

On the old grade school readers, the Dick and Jane books, the principal players were pictured on the book cover. There stood Dick and Jane with an open book, reading. As a child, I closely examined that cover and discovered that it clearly pictured the book from which they were reading. It was the same Dick and Jane book I then held in my hands, with the same Dick and Jane, standing, reading on yet another cover from yet another Dick and Jane book. On that smaller book, the one in their hands, was still another Dick and Jane book, and then another, on and on. Try as I might, I could not see where it stopped, and in my innocence I supposed it didn't. Who can say that it did? It was easier then for me to believe in the beauty of the infinite, having neither the inclination nor the intellect to dispute it.

I know now, in my wisdom, that it was impossible for it to go on forever. At some point, printer's ink and artistic ability was finite and blended together in a blurred dot too small to see. My adult eyes see limitation that youth doesn't know exists. Sadly, the practical and the possible began to limit the limitless, and Dick and Jane became my neighbors, driving a Mercury to Montgomery Ward.

I have tried, perhaps less than successfully, to explain why baseball resembles life and why Little League is important. I've drawn conclusions that are, as I have said, clichés, but clichés are proverbs when they are filled with meaning. Only from experience do we create memory, and only with memory do we create meaning. Living and playing the game, child or adult, offers up opportunities fraught with disappointment, but they are disappointments resplendent with opportunity. To expect or accept one without the other is unfortunately impossible, though mightily tried.

I was out in the yard, where I often went when the cobwebs began to close me in, walking between a row of blue spruce and ponderosa pine that my wife, mother, and I had planted several years back. They had grown slowly at first, agonizingly, imperceptibly, then, almost overnight they grew several feet a year. They served as sentries, keeping the south winds away from the house. The breezy whispering of the long-needled pines brushed my arm as I edged close to them.

"Daaad!" a voice called to me from the porch. "Daaaad!" again. It was my daughter, and then appearing with her from around the clapboard siding, my son. They were armed and ready, gloves and bats in hand. They spotted me and, always competing, raced to my location.

"Will you play catch with us?" asked Chad.

"I get to bat first," said Mandi, presupposing approval and jumping the gun on a chance.

We set up among two cottonwoods and a maple tree in the front, natural bases. I pitched. We would play two-on-one, me perpetually on the defensive. One child was in the outfield while the other batted. Three outs to an inning and ghosts permitted as base runners so the batter could extend his or her rally. It was a game we had played since we could play, and we played it like it mattered. Sometimes darkness would end it, or dinner, or maybe a phone call from a client, or sometimes it would end in a tie engineered by a catch or a throw, allowing the game to pick up tomorrow where it left off today.

That evening we played on uninterrupted. Each inning we edged closer to the end, but each inning went on. First Mandi was ahead, then Chad, and it seemed the last at bat was the decisive one, so the other child would plead for another inning, and we would all agree, not wanting it to end and caring little about the score.

It was late summer, and I knew I was going away. Perhaps, just perhaps, they did too. So we played on endlessly against the odds, fighting the dusky darkness until we could barely see the balls hit and pitched. Realizing someone could get hurt, I called an end to it. The sun having set, we walked together toward home, where my wife waited at the front door. The amber glow of the light behind her etched her silhouette onto the porch and out into the dry grass where we walked. I gave my glove to Chad, the ball to Mandi, and put my arms around their shoulders. We walked slowly, drinking in the night and the game like cold well water.

I stopped at the edge of my wife's shadow, and my children went on ahead, through the doorway and out of my sight. I wondered then, as I wonder now, about Dick and Jane and the book cover. I wondered if it really does go on forever, even if you can't see it.

18

MAKING THE CUT

Far better it is to dare mighty things, to win glorious triumphs, even though checkered by defeat, than to take rank with that poor soul who neither enjoys much nor suffers much, because he lives in that gray twilight that knows not victory nor defeat.

Theodore Roosevelt

We pretend to forgive failure, really we celebrate it. Bonehead Merkle lives forever and Bill Mazeroski's home run fades.

Donald Hall, *The Baseball Card Engagement Book*

It is a distinguishing feature of Little League that everyone makes the team, some team, if they try out. I like that, for in its egalitarianism it promotes opportunity at a time in the lives of young children when opportunity most needs promoting. There are no severed chances, cut down like mowed grass by the sickle of success, where only the Darwinians are left standing. Children, particularly susceptible to the crushing weight of rejection, can at least know that despite their talent level, they will have a home—teammates and a team.

Too soon, in other venues, the dross gets separated by adult expectations, where the ideal begins to shape the formation of the team. Boys and girls are shuttled off into alleys leading different places. Too soon, the positions on a team, like commodities rare and precious, are clamored for by a number greater than there are spaces available, leaving many disappointed.

Nothing like rancor colors my rhetoric. It is a natural and wholly American process that requires children, growing into adults, to prove their mettle in order to earn themselves a spot, and of this, too, I approve. For without this, competitive fires essential to improvement would not burn as bright. Potential loss drives desire like a prairie fire drives wildlife; panicky, yet alert and consistent, inexorable toward conclusion. Failure to react to the pressure means sure failure.

Little League, then, with its open-arms policy, is a last respite between the warm comfort of acceptance and the cold reality of rejection. Knowing this, we must strive to make the transition at once both less comforting and less rejecting, less warm and less cold.

The best thing about Little League is that in its natural state, it is played as a game. Unaltered by the hands and minds of adults, it is played for fun, and in that, can be played by any child, each skill adapting to each team, blended and bundled together. It is, at its simplest, a classroom, and teaching is its primary motive. Winning has not yet become its master, although one begins to wonder at Williamsport, site of the Little League World Series. On the myriad fields across this country where small boys and girls gather, skills are taught and learned easily and not so easily. The game is played for fun by children who have not yet forgotten what it is.

It was in a yard turned ballfield where I first learned about effort. Skinny, scrawny, and awkward, I was often the last kid chosen. I could throw okay, but I ran like I was my sister and didn't hit too well. About the best thing you could say about me was that I wasn't easily discouraged, though I had plenty of opportunities. In the mirror of my reminiscence, I find myself searching diligently, but without much luck, for successes. I was not very good.

Playing on a team filled with talent masked my deficiency. Squeezed between real hitters in a lineup, my groundout went unnoticed. Dropped innocently into the field, my errors were forgiven by the overachievement of my teammates. My misgiven play was redeemed, but there began to burn in me the hope and the desire to end the comedy in which I was the lead player. Driven by older brothers, I played, took grounders until my legs were darkly marked, caught fly balls until I could, and slowly climbed up the ladder of respectability.

With each play in a real game my skills became more acute. Even then, where others improved effortlessly, or so it seemed, my progress

was slow and ponderous. Every fly ball I caught, I believed I wouldn't. Every base hit I hit, I believed I couldn't. Driven by fear of failure, I jumped into the bottomless pool of effort and dog-paddled for days, barely staying above water.

It was not pretty. I was not blessed with grace. My play, instead, was encumbered, edgy, and persistent. What I could not do with my body, I learned to do with guile and smarts. What I could not do with guile, I learned to do by persistence. A fumbled ball wasn't an error if you made the throw to first in time. I learned that expecting too much too soon often disappoints, and it was better to play without quitting on each and every play; the results would take care of themselves.

To be sure, there were defeat and disappointment. My Little League years were replete with second best and should'a beens. As I, like all children, edged away from the game and into the purely competitive spirit of sport, I left behind me more losses than wins, more defeat than victory, more failure than success. And I learned much from those times, when, despite the effort, the reward was unreached.

It was 1963. It was the summer before my sixth grade. Later that fall, on a gray November day, I would lose my innocence (although I would not know I had lost it until years later) when Mrs. Buss would walk into our room, wiping tears from her eyes, to announce that the president had been shot. We would gather in the auditorium and listen to Walter Cronkite, normally solid as a rock, break down momentarily as he told us that our president was dead. I can still recall a look in his eyes that said that he, too, had lost something, and I wondered what. Basking in the warmth of the lazy summer sun, I did not know that soon the absolute rightness that I had supposed was America would be left lying in the mud of autumn like the broken gauntlet of a fallen hero. Baseball was all that mattered.

We played, unaware of our futures and unconcerned with our pasts. What mattered was today and the game. Tomorrow was as distant as the horizon—we trusted it would be there but cared little to explore it until it came. They were days of Mays and Mantle and Maris, and of Aaron, the man who would quietly overtake Ruth in numbers but never in fame. These were the days before Vietnam, and we looked no further than down the street to the ballfield, seeing only what we wanted to see.

I played on a team in Lincoln that had no name, only a number. Imagination was at a premium then, and numbers served us as well as names and mascots. Today, no self-respecting kid would play on a team called simply "6" or "3." Today they have flashy monikers given by men more interested in style than substance. My team was team *3,* and I, knowing no better, was proud to be there.

The league was called Little Chiefs, a variant of Little League. We played in the small ballparks across the town. Everyone got to play, and we played until one team won. We had fun. We wore our red hats to church as easily as to games, and our T-shirts left our scrawny backs only when our moms snuck them off us for a washing.

We were a tribe, young boys raised with *Leave It to Beaver,* gregarious and shy, large and small, separated geographically into units by street signs and school districts, but a tribe held together, nonetheless, by a sense of sameness, a unity of experience that we all felt and enjoyed. At the end of each season, all the teams would picnic at a local park, and our numbers spilled together easily and with a careless ambivalence. We got reacquainted with each other before school started again and pushed us together into a routine less to our liking.

Perhaps age has softened the lens through which I view that time. Perhaps, in my present circumstances, any field even remotely green looks greener. Perhaps—but I don't think so. I believe things have changed, times have turned, but the 1963 Little Chiefs still resembles its thirty-three-year-older cousin. We are unable to see the changes as we are carried along, bubbling over in a cauldron of consequence, carried along ever forward, rushing, expanding, and contracting, until we are either cast out, or consciously step away from the path on our own, long enough to look aside and askance and see what we once were and what we have now become.

At twelve, as my daughter is twelve, and at fourteen, as my son is fourteen, I was then what they are now. I played ball like they play ball. I caught flies like they catch flies. I made outs like they make outs. Smallish, stumbling, clumsily, I moved forward in childlike bliss, guarded by adults in a world going awry.

Throughout history it has been like this—short periods of peace in which children feel safe. We as a people travel along until an event, often hidden, comes along to disrupt our lives, enveloping us all only when we see and understand, too late to prevent the damage. The world is always and steadily going awry. We see only what we want to see and ignore that which we know to exist but want to wish away.

In the summer of my sixth grade, I made the cut. In the summer of my daughter's, I missed it. Try as I might, I cannot yet explain, for I do not as yet understand, why I would miss the cut I should make, and make the cut I should miss.

Little Chiefs held a tournament at the end of the regular season. "All-stars" were chosen by a group of coaches to play in the tournament. Most of the players were selected on the basis of their skill displayed throughout the year, and they were obvious choices.

A few positions for the tournament were left open for tryouts. Any boy who wanted to fill one of the few remaining slots would report for a daylong camp. My baseball desire had not yet faded into the cool public pools or into family vacations to Yellowstone or Aunt Mary's, so I suited up, took my glove, and donned my felt fitted hat. I made my way to the field, crossing the lawns of neighbors and traveling down an alley lined with trash cans and littered with house cats perched on fence tops.

When I arrived, I was met by stares and a few "Heys" from the boys, who looked me over like a used car no one would finance. *Out of place, no way, not a chance,* I saw them thinking.

I sat silently on the ground, just one in the crowd, as the coaches explained the skills we would practice and what they were looking for. I listened to what they said about desire and catching and third base and hitting. I hoped to glean from them some clue that might give me an edge. We would field, run, bat, catch flies, and field some more. I was discouraged, for I could do none of these well. The coaches left us to warm up our arms. One boy, Apollo-like, sauntered confidently over to me.

"You ain't got a chance. I seen ya play." He laughed a small laugh and smiled a small smile that said he was right, and he turned away.

I said nothing. I had learned to be quiet and nonemotive, concealing myself. If I spoke and then failed, the failing would be doubly hard. So I said nothing.

I volunteered to catch since there were few of these boys who would, as it was a dirty, hard position that held little promise of glory. It was the kind of job I liked. I could hide myself in armor, see the whole field, and think before I acted, giving me a chance to shield my deficiencies.

For about an hour, while pitchers tried out, I took balls in my shins, feet, over my head, to the right and left, and thankfully, a few into my pud. It seemed that I went unnoticed, since the coaches were concentrating on the other half of the battery, and after all, I was just filling in—the real catchers had already been chosen for the team.

Later we split up for a scrimmage. One of the coaches, remembering me from earlier, told me to put on the equipment and catch again.

"Red," he said, not knowing my name but seeing the color of my hair. "Red! Suit up, you're catching."

I did not swing a bat or catch a fly that day; instead I labored in anonymity behind the mask and chest protector. When my turn came to bat, I was asked to substitute for the other team's catcher, who had stubbed his thumb on a foul tip and split his nail open. I caught both ways, and I was disconsolate over this turn of events. Yet my not batting could have been seen as a blessing, given my proficiency at that art. The game ended, and the coaches gathered in the dugout to make their selections to add to the tournament team.

The head coach was short and burly. He gathered us together, got down on one knee, and spoke to us in earnest. He told us what we knew but didn't want to hear. Too many boys, too few spots.

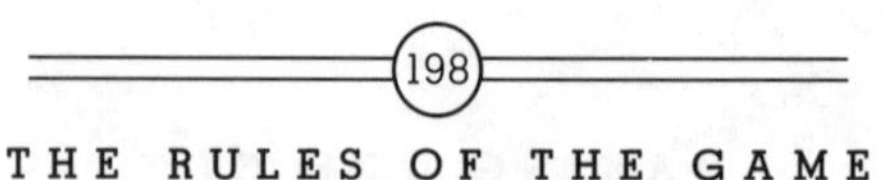

Proud of our effort. Some better than others. Learn from our mistakes. Always next year. I saw Apollo looking around for likely victims. His eyes met mine, and I wished I wasn't there.

The roll of names who had made the team was called alphabetically, which preempted surprise and cushioned the shock and disappointment as your letter passed by and your name wasn't called.

". . . Carson . . . Friedman . . . Gardner . . ." came the roll.

"Hohen-steen . . ." The rest of the names became a blur in my ears, like when you come up out of the deep end of the pool after a cannonball you laid into to splash the girls, and rising, hear only the muffled appreciation of your friends, applauding your mischief.

I lingered as other boys now wandered off. Apollo came over, shaking his head.

"You got lucky," he said, looking down.

I responded in the way young boys often do when they are forced into a corner. "Like heck I did."

And I understood then that the confidence comes when you do a job you are not expected to do and succeed in spite of your own limitations.

Thirty years later, a generation come and gone, I sit in the dugout, benched. I face the field again, looking inward. The successes of the past, the cuts made are now but dim shadows out of which look the hopes cf the future, haltingly, lacking confidence once again, afraid of the light.

Apollo baits me again, and as before, I am silent, knowing him to be right though wishing that it were not true.

"You ain't got a chance. I seen ya play."

I sit at my desk and look out my window at the short yard of gravel and brown grass, the concrete wall jutting up forebodingly, topped by swirls of barbed and razor wire that haughtily beckon, "Try me." From the gray sky snow is falling, indecisively and melting into the too warm earth. What imprisons me is myself—not the law, or the judge, or the institution. They are impostors, nothing more. The answers I seek about the character of my own soul evade me and mock my misery and the greater misery I have caused; they are recalcitrant, giving themselves up only after much struggle and only with much help.

I realize, like the children of Little League, that I cannot go it alone. Into my thoughts I wander as the snow outside finally accumulates into a thin blanket, pure and white on the dead and dying field. Apollo approaches again, laughing, convinced now more than ever, and tells me "You got lucky." With a glint of light peering up from under the blanket, I am left to wonder if he was right all along.

19

ON HITTING

When you play this game 20 years, go to bat 10,000 times, and get 3,000 hits, do you know what that means? You've gone 0 for 7,000.

Pete Rose,
as quoted by Joe Garagiolo in *It's Anybody's Ballgame*

The attempt and not the deed,
Confounds us.

William Shakespeare, *Macbeth*

As with many endeavors that seem simple, it is easier to write about hitting than do it. It is easier to do just about anything than it is to hit a baseball. Hitting is one effort where success occurring less than half the time is marveled at and celebrated.

Only one professional ballplayer in the last fifty years has ever batted above .400, that is, successfully hit the ball four times out of every ten attempts throughout the extended course of a baseball season. Ted Williams, a Red Sox ballplayer, did it through the front door, going 6 for 8 in a doubleheader on the last day of the regular season to finish at an astonishing .408, and that accomplishment alone would have marked him as one of the greatest hitters of all time, except that his usual and varied excellence had already given him away.

George Brett, recently retired stalwart of the Kansas City Royals, challenged that level in 1980, ending the season at .380, the highest mark of any recent player. Pete Rose, the all-time hitmeister, never came close. The Hall of Fame is replete with players whose skills were honed and excellent, but all faltered in the area of consistent hitting.

In any other profession, rebuke, not reward, would accompany such a standard. A doctor who saves four out of ten patients will soon find himself practicing some other art. A teacher who succeeds in advancing but four of ten students past their ABCs will not be high on the retention list. A politician who votes with the general opinion of his constituents four in ten times will have to spend an inordinate amount of money at election time to convince them to reelect him.

It is not a lowered standard that accepts this level of competence

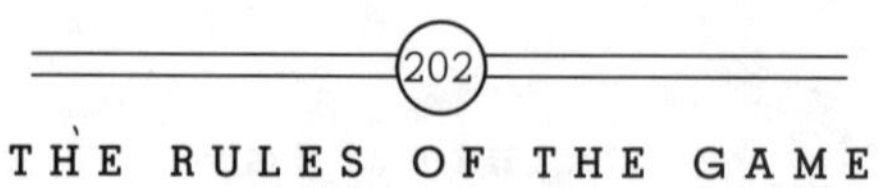

in baseball; rather, it speaks starkly of the brutal difficulty involved in hitting the ball. It is a task so genuinely difficult, so mystifying even to the experienced, that it has bred ritual, myth, and superstition to safeguard those who labor at it.

But put a twelve-year-old child in the box and listen to the chorus of disappointment when the hits don't come as regularly as the morning news. Think back, if you will, to the last time your child was at bat and came away empty. Your reaction? It is not an indictment of us all to say most parents, relatives, and friends expect from our children in that situation that which they cannot deliver.

Most unreasonable expectations are well intentioned. There is nothing malevolent about wanting our children to do well. One school of thought even argues that by setting expectations high you tend to encourage overachievement, and of course we all understand how valuable that personal trait is, especially to young and impressionable children. We naturally want our kids to achieve, to be the best—but in relation to what? We leave that question open ended and our aspirations for our children therefore become unanswerable, unattainable, and unachievable.

The waitress, young and partly unkempt, took the order from the men at the table, then after pausing to decipher her own handwriting, barked it out to the cook behind the wall.

"Two over easy, rack of hash and pork, two scrambled, hard, link and patty, one early riser special." Just as quickly, she slid the slip of paper she had held in her hand up into a clip attached to a circular metal rim that collected the orders of others waiting to eat.

The cafe was small and crowded. It was Saturday morning, and as if there were nothing else to do and nowhere else to do it, the wandering souls of this rural community—cast out of their own homes by cleaning wives and drawn by their recurrent desire to know each other's business—had gathered once again at this place. Wooden booths, worn smooth by the faded denim of customers, lined one wall. A short counter, covered with what was once fashionable Formica, formed an eating place for those alone. Round red stools stuck atop scratched silver pedestals lined the front of the counter, and from behind, unoccupied, looked preposterously classy in a woefully dressed down display.

Down the middle of the floor sat tables, round and square, bought at an auction when the Tip Top Tap went belly-up in the late seventies, forced out of business by high interest and a drinking owner. Each table was surrounded by an odd assortment of men, young and old, with an occasional youngster thrown in. They talked as they waited; they talked as they ate; they talked as they ordered more coffee from the waitress, who, working alone, wondered aloud more than once, "Where's JoAnne?" She rushed from table to table, too busy to become angry.

The men didn't talk about anything in particular but about everything in general. The subjects drifted at each table like a tumbleweed caught in a shifting wind, back and forth, then easily away, picked up by another table, and off again.

The waitress carried an order in both arms over to a table near the center of the cafe and laid it correctly around the men, who hungrily began to eat. Last night, the kids had played a ballgame in

the annual summer team tournament, and they would play again tonight. These men were fathers of sons and sons of fathers.

One of the men stopped and washed his food down with a large gulp of coffee.

"Ada!" he said, pulling back from the cup. "This coffee is hot!"

The waitress, used to this, answered walking away, "Can't brew it without gettin' it hot." The men at the table laughed between their eggs and hash, acknowledging with nods the truth of her reply.

"Quite a game last night," said a man dressed for work in blue denim and a light, short-sleeved chambray shirt that let his biceps bulge out of the ends of the sleeves. The other men stopped and looked up.

"Ya know, Ed," said another, setting his slightly burnt toast on the edge of his plate, "I don't understand how the boys could blow a six-run lead! It shouldn'ta even been close."

"Pitchin'," Ed answered.

"When we was playin', we could finish a game. We'da never let 'em back in it." Neil punctuated the self-assured comment with a gulp of coffee.

"If ya can't hold 'em with a six-run lead, somethin's wrong with your pitchin'." Ed acted as if no one had heard him. "Them boys gotta learn not to take a lead for granted. No killer instinct."

The conversation turned back the clock to days of youth vaguely recalled, refashioned, re-created by aging men. "When we was playing . . . we'da done it different. . . . No way they'da come back on us. . . . We had a team. . . ." And on and on, accurate only to the extent imagined.

The competitive comparison rose like a leviathan and scourged

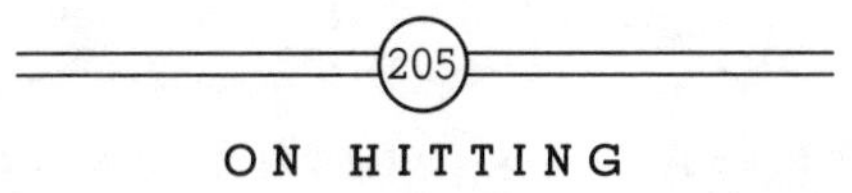

the remembrance. At that cafe table, no boy could measure up to the memory of his father's effort; no boy would be accepted for doing less than memory expected.

"Y'all remember our game against the Indians in the district play-offs?" said Ed, half-asking, half-telling. "We had a lead in the bottom of the sixth. Banks was pitchin' . . ."

"He's gonna be back for the reunion in June," interrupted Neil.

"Really? Where's he at anyway? California?" asked another.

"Arizona. Tucson, I think." Neil stopped, anxious for Ed to continue.

"Well, we had the lead," continued Ed, "and Coach Bisk told Banks, 'I ain't takin' you out, no matter what.' Well, Banks knows that Bisk means it. It's all up to him, so he hauls off and throws nine straight heaters, darn near burnt a hole in the catcher's hand. . . ."

"Who was catchin'? Flanders?" asked Neil.

"No, Flanders sat out that game. 'Twas Jefferies."

"Oh, yeah."

"His hand hurt so bad afterward he stuck it in the water cooler just to ice it down. Anyway, Banks throws nine straight heaters right down the pipe! Not one of those Indians even saw 'em. Blew it right by 'em. That was pitchin'!"

"There ain't been a pitcher in this town like Banks since then. Them boys don't even know what pitchin' is compared to him."

Generally nodded agreement circled the table, like the heads of small poodle figurines in the rear windows of old cars.

"They don't pitch like Banks did–not anymore," was the consensus.

But Banks, late of Tucson, remembered now only for nine straight

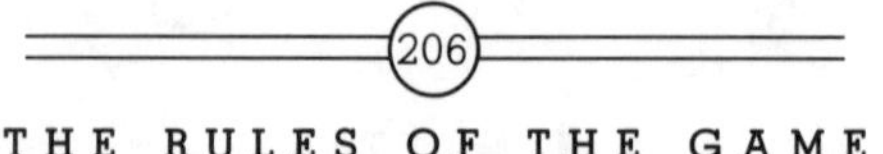

strikes, walked more than he struck out, and won only seven games that year. J. C., who pitched until relieved in last night's game, had won sixteen that year and had struck out about eight a game. He was stronger, faster, and better. He had every advantage except that of distance—distance in time from actual achievements, which are enhanced in the remembering. The men talked as if a reverse law of evolution was in effect: Older is better, and the new models are somehow inferior. Banks couldn't have hit .400 if his life depended on it.

We so very much want our own children to hit it out of the park. It is not for me to say what you should feel or expect in that regard. Each of you must answer it for yourself and with your own. As for me, my children can hit the ball with the best of them, but that is no longer my measure of success. That is not my standard for appraisal, for unless I have hit flawlessly, I cannot expect perfection in them. They cannot live the dreams I have dreamed. My wishes, hopes, and expectations for them must remain my own, lest they overcome me and then them and create that which was not meant to be.

It is a natural parental desire to want our children to be the best and, where we have succeeded, to follow in our footsteps. But being natural does not make it right. Each child must make his or her own success: following someone else's path creates only a follower, and sooner or later the path will end or veer off or lead elsewhere and lose them in the mirage of someone else's expectation.

For each child who bats and misses and learns that failing to hit

is part of learning to hit, we have created in that child an opportunity for lasting success.

Hitting is a difficult art. Even more difficult is letting your child try and miss and fail and learn that in the effort lies the merit.

I prefer my children to enter the box, get comfortable with their own stance, pick their own pitch, and take their best cut. If in doing that they go 0 for 7000, they at least will have learned their own lesson, not mine. And it is in that learning where memories worth remembering are made.

20

THE RULES OF THE GAME

There once was an umpire whose vision,
Was cause for abuse and derision.
He remarked in surprise,
"Why pick on my eyes?
It's my heart that dictates my decision."

Ogden Nash, "An Ump's Heart"

He brought an eye for all he saw;
He mixt in all our simple sports;
They pleased him, fresh from brawling courts
And dusty purlieus of the law.

Alfred Lord Tennyson,
"In the Valley of the Cauteretz"

As much as we conceive of Little League as magical, boundless and unrestrained, it is not. The game is defined and determined by rules. Little League is a game played to build character and teach lessons. The rules of the game create an order without which the game becomes unmanageable and meaningless.

To observe the innards of baseball, a dissection of the game and the intricate web of rules is unnecessary, because this game routinely plays itself inside out. The exposure bodes well for understanding.

The rules that children learn to follow are not as difficult to understand as they are to explain. Take, for instance, the rule about base runners advancing on a fly ball. If a fly ball is caught, any runner who leaves his base to advance to another must do so only after tagging up and after the fly is caught. In other words, don't leave your base until the ball is caught. If you do, a fielder who throws the ball behind you to the fielder on the base from which you advanced too early will tag you out, and you will look foolish.

This rule has two main characteristics all rules of value possess: clear explanation and clear consequence. Only in the implementation is there any judgment—when did he leave, when did he return—and it is not in the execution but in the judgment that the rule is ever in controversy. The argument in implementation comes not in understanding, but in observing, so it is the eye rather than the word that is questioned. While we curse the rule, we really mean to curse the judge who implements it. The rule, after all, just sits there, and if we don't like it, we have the power to change it or revoke it if we wish. It is our servant, we its master.

Being human, we do not like to admit we are wrong. It is easier

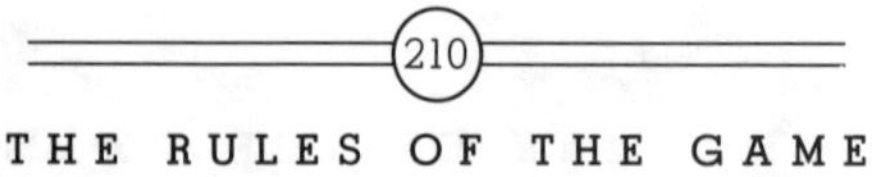

to acknowledge the fallibility of the mirror than the image. Little League, played on a stage with open disclosure, hides little and reveals much. The mistakes that we make, we make out in the great wide open, and few like to fail. But even fewer like to fail in the open arena. Better the mistake be made in the darkness, where sight is dimmed and memories foggy, than under the open scrutiny of an interested world.

That is why, in one sense, Little League is so appealing. In order to live through your own failure you must accept that you are fallible; in order to accept your fallibility, you must learn to recognize your own failure. A mistake guarded by the darkness does little but build a false domicile of pride in your heart and soul that will not admit the entrance of humility and humanity.

We seek, as adults, parents, and coaches, to teach lessons we want our children to learn. Yet how can we teach that which we ourselves fail to understand? Is it, we ask in retrospection, the height of hypocrisy to teach the lessons of the game and give lip service to the rules, yet follow them ourselves only when it suits our purposes? This lesson is perhaps the essence of all that is valuable and worthwhile in Little League. Boiled down to its barest, it simply means that we should not expect our children to act substantially different than we ourselves act. If we teach the good we know but unteach it by example, we do damage to both the education and the student.

When I played ball I never learned what I needed to know. True, I learned the fundamentals: how to catch, how to throw, how to hit. I learned the techniques and the situational playmaking I needed to understand how to play the game and play it well. I learned the rules of the game—that is, I understood what they meant and how they were applied and articulated, and even on occasion misapplied in a variety of situations.

I believed that even though the rules were in black and white, they were little but guidelines since discretion and subjective judgment colored their application. But even then, I accepted them as necessary for order and structure.

On occasion, a rule was misapplied or a rule was followed but stretched taut. That, too, for me, became part of the rules. In their application, the rules themselves become participants, active role players who helped or hurt—the way a south wind pushing moist air over a cold front, dropping rain or hail, helps or hurts the fawning crop. Once we start the game, we cannot change the rules—we must live with them and by them or face the consequences. No one is bigger than the smallest rule book.

When I was young, I played the game until I was called away. I didn't know the limitation of innings or time. It wasn't all that important who won, and therefore the game went on until, one by one, we were picked off by our mothers or fathers or by chores undone or brought home by hunger or decimated by our thinned ranks for any of a hundred reasons.

My son, Chad, will quit only if he's ahead. My daughter, Mandi, learning that neat trick from him, will extend the game forever until her mother calls her in. Yet even in those pickup games, though the rules are sculpted to fit the geography of an unusual field or the physiology of a small-fry or heavy hitter, they still stand undaunted, guardians of the integrity of the game, and they are ultimately accepted by all who play the game.

Still, acceptance does not mean adherence, for while one requires understanding, the other requires both understanding and a conscious effort to learn and follow. That means an effort involving greater sacrifice and smaller pride. It inevitably contrasts with our innate nature, which scorns sacrifice and cherishes pride.

We humans learn the rules not to adhere to them, but to push up against them. This challenge to the rules is not a new phenomenon; it can be traced to the beginnings of man. Perhaps it is learned behavior, for some of our brightest and most learned do it better than most.

If breaking the rules is a learned behavior, then I am fearful. For if it is a learned behavior, that means we learn it from others and teach it to our own. We take a deduction for the clothes we give to charity, knowing full well they are worthless, and we are able to pay fewer taxes because of it. Our sons and daughters lead off of first before the pitch is thrown, steal second, and are rewarded instead of being called out. We stop at a supermarket, and in receiving too much change, we pocket it in surreptitious glee and convince ourselves that that is their problem, not ours. Our sons and daughters settle under a fly ball, bobble it to the ground, then grab it quickly and hold it up like they found a diamond. They save the out but lose their innocence, and we cheer their cleverness and agile deception.

We are hidden behind a power that can control disclosure and a conscience that can convince itself that black is white and wrong is right. And when our children act as we act, we wonder aloud where we went wrong. We wring our hands and gnash our teeth, but we look only at our children, and seeing our reflection, we turn away from that mirror of indictment.

It is time, at least for me, to face that mirror. Perhaps long past time. I can no longer turn my eyes away and ignore my reflection, because it burns brighter and hotter than the image itself. Faced with a choice of ignorance or pain, I choose pain. Pain will go away; ignorance lasts forever. Better that I know and face my condition, however painful, than live in ignorance. The rules, as they always do, as they should do, have risen up and thrown me out, and I sit on the sidelines, behind the wall, and wonder if I may ever play the game again.

Summer has drifted lazily into the autumn coolness, and autumn now likewise has gone south for the winter. The ground is cold and hard and unforgiving; it plays no favorites, treating us all with equal ambivalence. Soon, ever so soon, the warming sun's rays will glance down over the tilting earth and heat awaken the dormant, creating a sweet green carpet to cover the Little League field where once we played.

There is no way to promise this will happen, yet I am assured of it, as sure as I am that after night comes morning and after life comes death. It is a welcome constant in our lives. We can believe it will happen because it has happened that way so many times before.

Something quite human carries us through the winters of our Little League years—the winters where failed dreams are forgotten and new dreams and goals surpass the last. Winters where singles become doubles, and doubles triples, and our averages soar above the low ceiling of our limitations. Where kids who can't hit, hit; where kids who can't field, field; where kids who can't run, run like the wind; and kids who can't play, play like they've never played before. The winter snows smother our past errors, and solstice hope melts away the limits they've imposed. We believe on faith and we return on hope. We return to the fields and parks and grassy arenas of our youth to learn and relearn and to unmake mistakes we have harbored silently in the cold.

Faith gives us another chance when all our tickets have been punched, another trip on the journey of unknown destination. We have a choice to either get on or stay off, and we take a chance only by not standing still. We know where we will be if we abandon faith, stand silently off to the side, and watch the train pass by. The boarding pass of hope puts us on the trip to brighter fields and greener greens and places where the stitched sphere is whiter than purity itself. It is our choice to again play the game, to allow it to offer the redemption we seek, though it makes no guarantees.

My children are now what I once was. They play the game that I once played. The rules of the game will guide them as they once guided me. I like that, but it scares me. There is treasure in generational ritual, and baseball is nothing if not that. But there is danger there too. For if the ritual is askew, having been misused or badly practiced, what will prevent it from being wrongly learned by those still learning? Perhaps the best I can say is that it was not the game that failed me, but I, it. And the rules are not made to be broken but to be followed.

As we began, a game is again being played. It goes on endlessly, inning after inning, season after season. This year I watch. My children manage without me. This year I'll toss no balls with them and catch no flies. And I won't be there to dust off their dirty backsides after a safe slide into home.

The game won't stop in my absence—it will barely miss me, but that, too, that studied disregard of personality the game exhibits in its truest form, is an asset. The game goes on with new participants, and old ones step aside or fall aside, or are put aside, rarely noticed or missed. The hope that breathes new life into the game each year carries you along even when you are forgotten, and remembers you to the ancient ritual that passes, bloodlike, between fathers and sons and mothers and daughters and all who would be children again, if they could.

If I understood them, I could better explain the mysteries of the game, the lessons of Little League. I am only able to say what I know, and even that changes as I come to realize that I can only state that with each new inning we can learn anew. What we once thought was knowledge is no longer as we move forward into the unknown that we once feared but now welcome, our own extra inning.

No matter what, despite the errors made, the game goes on. And I long for the day when I don my glove, leave the bench, trot off into the great green living expanse of an open outfield, and play a game of catch with my kids.

ACKNOWLEDGMENTS

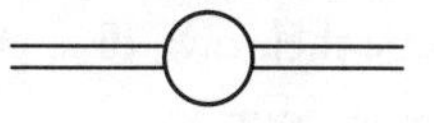

Much time has passed since I began writing *The Rules of the Game* from the cloistered confines of my cell at the maximum security prison in Lincoln where I began my sentence on October 1, 1993. From where I am housed now, I can still look across a field of soybeans to the west, down a ravine where the sweat lodge sits next to a small tree-lined lake, then up again to the hill on which sits the stark, pale white concrete walls of LCC. I wonder daily about the lives of the men inside that abyss and pray that they can know in some small way what I took from that place and what it took from me.

I have met new friends and lost old ones. I have become reacquainted with my family in a way unlike any other and have come to understand and deeply appreciate what they mean to me. I have faced my own demons and have learned what it means to be haunted, and how, with faith, to keep the ghosts in check. I have come to a deep, personal, and painful understanding of what I meant to people, and how much damage my misdeeds did to others.

I fear I will leave someone out in thanking those who have been with me. If I do, please forgive me. It was the small gesture of a quiet friend that kept me going forward when dark days came, and I thank those who helped me sincerely. Especially to those friends back home who overcame their own disappointment and offered me their hand, I am forever in your debt.

To my newfound friends at LCC and CCL who decided I was okay after all and then gave me their friendship, support, and confidence, I say much obliged. To Lonnie and Waylon, who let me listen to the Husker games through a grate in the wall when a grate in the wall was all I had, thanks. To Keith, who painted with me and laughed with me, then understood what I was and came to realize what he could become, many thanks. To Brian and Patty Rodwell, who lived through the hell of a wrongful conviction and became my close friends, trust that your day will come too.

To Danny, Shane, Stacy, Scott, Brian, JJ, Carlos, Steve, Kody, Tim, Randy, Bryon, Ritchey, Doug, Gary, Dennis, Jim, Rick, John, Taggart, Pam, Regina, Marsha, OB, Shawn, Jason, Roberta, and the countless others whose lives overlapped mine here, know that knowing you meant something to me.

Special thanks to Laurie, who always smiled and gave her special kind of encouragement to others even when it wasn't in her best interest—you're some kind of okay to me.

A few people you meet in here are better than they will ever be able to show. To Martin Vega, thanks. You got nothing coming, but you give a little every day.

To Wes, I know what you have gone through and felt. Thanks for being a friend.

To Staff, Smitty, Fish, Higgins, and Barbara at CCL and to Doni and the group at the YY, knowing that your job wasn't made easier by who I was, I appreciate the treatment you gave me.

Some people never learn, and I am grateful for second chances. To my good friend and an extraordinary farmer, Dave Ludtke, Professor John Gradwohl, Senator Ernie Chambers, Professor John Wunder, Professors Winkle and Coble, Ed Russo, Mari Crispin, and the others who encouraged my attempt to start over then helped me do it, my eternal gratitude. To Senator Dwite Pederson, who came by when almost no one else would and kept coming, you know how I feel. You are a good man and a good friend.

Few people realize how alone alone is until they walk their soul around an empty room. Pastor Brogaard, Pastor Leeper, Pastors Ebert and Borcherding, the faith families at The House of New Life, Redeemer, Hope, and St. Paul, my family at Grace Lutheran churches, and stalwart Christian volunteers, Lois and Martin Bauer, all helped me realize that with God no room is ever empty. Chaplain Carlberg came to me on his first day, and his gentle, compassionate common sense and faith lifted me when I was lowest. Bob, you are a wonderful healer.

My family wondered, and may wonder still, but they stood by me, and that means I can be welcomed back. William, Sarah, and Jack; James, Doug, and Vicki, I know that it has not been easy. I hope that you will be proud again. Aunt Elaine, while some may be bigger, none has a bigger heart. Your happy cards and notes always came to me at exactly the right time.

To my ballplayers back home, who are grown and growing, I will always consider you my boys. Every minute I was coaching you was a joy. If I said anything unkind, then or now, know that I meant well. I love you guys.

Neil Kaup, Ed Briscoe, Ron Rolfes, and Roger Thompson were the coaches who shaped my desire to never, never give up. It is not in the getting knocked down but in the getting up that real achievement lies. Thanks for the hand up you gave me years ago.

To Shane, my appreciation for never giving up the ghost—on me or yourself. I wish I could've been there but was glad you were nonetheless.

To Jay and Chloe, my thanks. You were there from the beginning and stayed until the end. Not many else did, and your Christian concern was invaluable to my spiritual sanity. So I got that going for me, which is nice.

My editors at Thomas Nelson, Lonnie Hull DuPont and Sheryl Taylor, took my manuscript and lovingly crafted out of it this book. They made me sound better than I am and left the heart of the book alone. It is a rare talent that can perform surgery without drawing blood. You done good.

To my agent and friend, Lawrence Jordan, who gave me some hope and good news by his faith in this book, my heartfelt thanks. I will meet you personally sometime soon and thank you more appropriately. Until then, know that your faith has allowed me to say things that would have otherwise gone unsaid. This book is as much yours as mine.

To Kathy—saying I'm sorry won't cut it. Maybe this book will help. Thanks for being a good mother to Chad and Mandi when they needed it most. My best to you always.

I cannot say that living through my sentence has been much fun,

Mom and Dad, but in these waning years we have together, it has given me, and you also, I hope, something we did not always have: honesty and love. That has meant everything to me. My thanks and eternal love to you both.

Not many men are given children like the ones I've been blessed with. Those days when I felt sorry for my lot and wanted to quit, I needed only to look at your pictures on my wall and remember how wonderfully good I've got it. Nothing is as valuable or important as the treasure of your love and the hope of our eventual reunion. I wrote this book for you and want you to know it was hard to write—it's even harder to be apart. Never stop fighting until the fight is done. I love you both and always will.

About the Author

Kurt Hohenstein was born in Lincoln, Nebraska. He lived on the family farm near Homer, Nebraska, after earning his bachelor and juris doctorate degrees from the University of Nebraska. He is presently pursuing his master's and doctorate degrees in history.

Kurt currently resides at Community Corrections Center-Lincoln, where he enjoys an occasional game of catch with his kids.